Cambridge Elements

Elements in Corpus Linguistics
edited by
Susan Hunston
University of Birmingham

LEXICAL MULTIDIMENSIONAL ANALYSIS

Identifying Discourses and Ideologies

Tony Berber Sardinha
Pontifical Catholic University of São Paulo

Shannon Fitzsimmons-Doolan
Texas A&M University – Corpus Christi

Shaftesbury Road, Cambridge CB2 8EA, United Kingdom

One Liberty Plaza, 20th Floor, New York, NY 10006, USA

477 Williamstown Road, Port Melbourne, VIC 3207, Australia

314–321, 3rd Floor, Plot 3, Splendor Forum, Jasola District Centre, New Delhi – 110025, India

103 Penang Road, #05–06/07, Visioncrest Commercial, Singapore 238467

Cambridge University Press is part of Cambridge University Press & Assessment, a department of the University of Cambridge.

We share the University's mission to contribute to society through the pursuit of education, learning and research at the highest international levels of excellence.

www.cambridge.org
Information on this title: www.cambridge.org/9781009598439

DOI: 10.1017/9781009335683

© Tony Berber Sardinha and Shannon Fitzsimmons-Doolan 2025

This publication is in copyright. Subject to statutory exception and to the provisions of relevant collective licensing agreements, no reproduction of any part may take place without the written permission of Cambridge University Press & Assessment.

When citing this work, please include a reference to the DOI 10.1017/9781009335683

First published 2025

A catalogue record for this publication is available from the British Library

ISBN 978-1-009-59843-9 Hardback
ISBN 978-1-009-33569-0 Paperback
ISSN 2632-8097 (online)
ISSN 2632-8089 (print)

Additional resources for this publication at www.cambridge.org/Berber

Cambridge University Press & Assessment has no responsibility for the persistence or accuracy of URLs for external or third-party internet websites referred to in this publication and does not guarantee that any content on such websites is, or will remain, accurate or appropriate.

Lexical Multidimensional Analysis

Identifying Discourses and Ideologies

Elements in Corpus Linguistics

DOI: 10.1017/9781009335683
First published online: January 2025

Tony Berber Sardinha
Pontifical Catholic University of São Paulo

Shannon Fitzsimmons-Doolan
Texas A&M University – Corpus Christi

Author for correspondence: Tony Berber Sardinha, tonycorpuslg@gmail.com

Abstract: *Lexical multidimensional analysis* (LMDA), an extension of Biber's (1988) multidimensional analysis, seeks to identify dimensions (sets of correlated lexical features across texts in a corpus), unveiling underlying patterns of lexical co-occurrence and variation within texts that are operationalized as a variety of latent, macro-level discursive constructs. Initially developed in the 2010s, LMDA has been applied to diverse domains, including education policy, national representations, applied linguistics, music, the infodemic, religion, sustainability, and literary style. This Element introduces LMDA for the identification and analysis of discourses and ideologies, offering insights into how lexis marks discourse formations and ideological alignments. Two case studies demonstrate the application of LMDA: uncovering discourses on climate change within conservative social media and analyzing ideological discourses in migrant education texts.

Keywords: corpus linguistics, ideologies, discourses, multidimensional analysis, lexical system

© Tony Berber Sardinha and Shannon Fitzsimmons-Doolan 2025

ISBNs: 9781009598439 (HB), 9781009335690 (PB), 9781009335683 (OC)
ISSNs: 2632-8097 (online), 2632-8089 (print)

Contents

1 Introduction   1

2 Synthesizing Existing LMDA Scholarship   13

3 How to Conduct a Lexical Multidimensional Analysis   26

4 Case Study 1: The Discourses Around Climate Change on
  a Conservative Social Media Platform   33

5 Case Study 2: Exploring the Distribution of Selected
  Migrant Education Ideological Discourses Over Time
  and Register   52

6 Conclusion   74

  References   76

1 Introduction
1.1 General Introduction

In this Element, we introduce lexical multidimensional analysis (LMDA), an extension of the multidimensional (MD) analysis framework developed by Biber in the 1980s ("multi-feature multidimensional analysis") to study register variation. Through the identification of (lexical) dimensions or sets of correlated lexical features, LMDA enables the analysis of lexical patterning from a multidimensional perspective. These lexical dimensions represent a variety of latent, macro-level discursive constructs. Although LMDA can be utilized for a range of lexis-based analyses, in this Element the focus is on its application to discourse analysis for the exploration of discourses and ideologies.

The authors have independently developed LMDA since the 2010s, initially through Fitzsimmons-Doolan's analysis of language ideologies in a body of educational policy texts (Fitzsimmons-Doolan, 2014, 2019) and Berber Sardinha's analysis of representations of American and Brazilian cultures on Google Books (Berber Sardinha, 2014, 2019, 2020). Since then, the approach has been extended to the analysis of other topics and domains, including US migrant education (Fitzsimmons-Doolan, 2023), the historical development of applied linguistics (Berber Sardinha, 2021, 2022a), popular music (Delfino et al., 2023), the infodemic (Berber Sardinha et al., 2023), and literary style (Kauffmann & Berber Sardinha, 2021), among other domains.

In this Element, we introduce readers to LMDA by focusing on theoretical and operational issues inherent in this approach. On a theoretical level, we explore the relationship of lexis to discourse and ideologies by discussing how lexis serves as markers of discourse formations and ideological alignment. On an operational level, we provide initial guidance on technical issues, from handling frequency counts to the utilization of statistical procedures. Since LMDA includes qualitative analysis of texts, we offer insights into interpreting sets of correlated lexical features from a discourse analytical standpoint.

Two case studies are included to demonstrate the practical application of LMDA in analyzing discourses in different contexts. The first case study illustrates how LMDA can reveal the discourses surrounding climate change on the conservative GETTR social media platform, providing insights into how these discourses manifest in a contested space. And the second case study examines migrant education ideological discourses, focusing on their distribution over time and by register.

1.2 LMDA's Foundation in Traditional Multidimensional Analysis

Procedurally and theoretically, LMDA is grounded in traditional MD analysis (TMDA). Douglas Biber developed MD analysis in the mid 1980s (Biber, 1988) for the functional description of variation across multiple registers, which, according to Biber and Conrad (2004, p. 42), are "different varieties of language that are associated with different situations and purposes." Since then, MD analysis has evolved to address single-register analysis, including examining variation by authors, social groups, or time periods. As such, the primary goal of TMDA is twofold: first, to identify the intrinsic linguistic parameters, or dimensions, that underlie variation (e.g., by register or style); and second, to delineate the linguistic similarities and differences among texts in relation to these dimensions along a continuous space of variation.

Typically, the basis for the interpretation of linguistic co-occurrence in TMDA is functional. According to Biber (1995, p. 30), "linguistic features co-occur in texts because they reflect shared functions." As a consequence, the dimensions resulting from the co-occurrence of the linguistic features will reflect the communicative functions performed by the texts in particular situational contexts.

Linguistic co-occurrence is captured statistically in TMDA through the computation of correlation coefficients for each pair of linguistic features across the texts in the corpus. Because each observation unit is an individual text, the correlation quantifies how pairs of linguistic features co-occur (positive correlation) or are mutually exclusive (negative correlation) across different texts. However, since in TMDA the association between linguistic co-occurrence and functional realization is predicated on groups of features performing communicative functions, rather than individual pairs of features, it is necessary to rely on multivariate statistical procedures to detect such patterns of association.

Factor analysis leads to the identification of the dimensions, which are the underlying parameters of variation across the texts. The factors are interpreted based on the communicative functions of the co-occurring features and given an interpretive label to capture their essence. Once interpreted communicatively, the factors are considered dimensions.

Since the dimensions represent a continuum of variation, registers can be systematically compared along the dimensions. The similarity between registers is determined by how similarly they use the features that co-occur within these dimensions. Since no single dimension can fully capture the range of similarities and differences among registers, a multidimensional conceptualization of register variation is needed.

The multidimensional nature of the approach is premised on the assumption that multiple parameters of variation act simultaneously on the texts, shaping them to perform a particular job in a particular communicative situation. This means that each single text reflects each dimension to a particular degree, and that no text is free from the incidence of any dimension. The extent to which a text is shaped by the incidence of a dimension is referred to as the extent of its markedness on a dimension. Consequently, different texts will be marked by different dimensions at varying degrees, resulting in a distinctive multidimensional profile of each text. Because functional variation among texts is largely predicted by register (Biber, 2012), texts from the same register will tend to have similar multidimensional profiles in TMDA.

The linguistic features used in TMDA are lexico-grammatical, predominantly comprising structural elements such as tense, aspect, subordination, phrasal structures, modalization, and coordination. Additionally, lexical features are categorized into grammatical classes (such as downtoners, hedges, amplifiers) or semantic categories that differentiate within word classes, including nouns (e.g., abstract, animate, technical), adjectives (e.g., color, evaluative, time), and verbs (e.g., communication, mental, existence). This feature set is selected for its ability to describe the underlying communicative parameters of language from a functional perspective. Though the procedures and underlying assumptions about variation are shared with TMDA, LMDA uses only lexical features and, thus, the resulting dimensions are theorized as macro-level discursive constructs such as discourses, ideologies, or themes.

1.3 Discourses and Ideologies

In contrast to TMDA which identifies functional variation in corpora, LMDA is a method for identifying a different type of variation in a corpus – namely that of latent, macro-level discursive structures. Among such structures, this Element focuses on discourses and ideologies, which we elaborate on in this subsection. We use *ideological discourses* as an umbrella term which includes a variety of constructs that exist in the "socio cognitive" space bounded by and between ideologies and "text or talk" (van Dijk, 2018, p. 242). Discourses (Baker, 2010), language ideologies (Kroskrity, 2004; Schieffelin et al., 1998), ideological discourses (Fitzsimmons-Doolan, 2023), and representations (Berber Sardinha, 2019, 2020) have all been identified in this space. Examples of entities identified under the umbrella of ideological discourses include assumed ideological positions such as *immigrants are threats, a people group shares a common language* (e.g., Germans speak German), and *growth is always desirable*. Other entities are less transparently ideological, such as *the discourse of educational practice.* When we use the term *ideological discourses* in this Element, we are referring to a range of macro-level discursive constructs that share many common features but can be distinguished on some parameters.

Ideological discourses can be expressed about a range of topics and, though usually highly recognizable as concepts in their explicit form, are rarely expressed explicitly. For our purposes, by ideological discourses, we mean socially shared, socially situated representations of real-world phenomena conveyed implicitly through language use. Because they are shared, ideological discourses also constrain or limit how real-world phenomena are represented. By socially situated, we mean that ideological discourses are developed through social practice and social experience. Because they represent real-world phenomena, ideological discourses make meaning.

Ideological discourses allocate social power (Kroskrity, 2004). They may also be thought of in terms of dominance. That is, when actions consistent with an ideological discourse are taken, some individuals benefit while others do not (or lose) in terms of resource allocation. Dominant discourses are widely accepted and naturalized (Kroskrity, 2004). They tend to be expressed and perceived as "facts." Nondominant discourses can be referred to as *resistant* or *alternative*.

As mentioned earlier, the entities of ideological discourses tend not to be expressed explicitly, but are identified with repeated patterns of wording (Stubbs, 1996, p. 158, 2001) or evaluative stances (Hunston, 2011). However, register differences also mean that these entities may be expressed differently in different texts (Berber Sardinha, 2021). Corpus linguistics studies are typically used to identify these patterns through measures of relative frequency, repetition, and association.

1.4 Corpus Linguistics Approaches to Ideological Discourses

In this subsection, we focus on two influential approaches to discourse analysis that have been integrated with corpus tools and methods to study ideological discourses: critical discourse analysis (CDA) and corpus-assisted discourse studies (CADS).

In the 1990s, CDA emerged as a distinct academic field, marking a development in the study of language and society. It is inherently interdisciplinary, drawing on a diverse array of disciplines including pragmatics, sociolinguistics, philosophy, social psychology, and theoretical linguistics. One of the primary objectives of CDA is to facilitate an intersectional dialog among these disciplines.

As a politically committed field (Caldas-Coulthard & Coulthard, 1996, p. xi), CDA assumes a proactive role in seeking social justice, aligning its analytical focus with the pursuit of equitable societal structures. As Forchtner (2013, p. 1439) puts it, CDA does not regard "discourse [as] merely talk," but rather as a constitutive phenomenon that "actually structures conduct" (Webster, 2003, p. 89). Across approaches, CDA scholars are committed to "de-mystifying ideologies and power through the systematic and retroductable investigation of semiotic data" (Wodak & Meyer, 2009, p. 3).

Although CDA is not a corpus-based approach, researchers have experimented with corpus methods, partly in response to methodological criticism concerning rigor and objectivity. A notable critique comes from Widdowson (1995), who contends that CDA analysts often conduct analyses with the primary aim of confirming their pre-existing hypotheses (e.g., by cherry-picking examples) rather than seeking to gather comprehensive evidence that could potentially contest their views. Similarly, Fowler (1996, p. 8) raises concerns about the scope of CDA, specifically its tendency to engage with a limited range of texts, resulting in evidence that is "fragmentary and exemplificatory." These criticisms stem from the qualitative nature of CDA, which demands deep and interpretative engagement with data, often at the expense of a broader sample size. Addressing the issue of limited text samples, Stubbs (1997) suggests incorporating large text samples into CDA, which can be achieved through various approaches, one of which is to utilize existing precompiled corpora as sources for extracting a more narrowly focused collection of texts that are relevant to the research objectives.

In applying corpus linguistics to CDA, researchers typically utilize tools like concordances, word frequency lists, and keywords. An example is Orpin (2005), who employed concordancing and word frequency counts in the analysis of the semantic domain of *corruption*. The study analyzed the frequencies of collocates of these words, using a corpus of 800 texts, sourced from four newspapers within the Bank of English.

Beyond frequency-based analysis for CDA studies using corpus linguistics, Stubbs (1997) proposes the adoption of methodological principles advocated by MD analysis. First, this would involve the recognition that "registers are very rarely defined by individual features, but consist of clusters of associated features which have a greater than chance tendency to co-occur" (Stubbs, 1997, p. 5). Second, this integration would involve adopting analyses "of co-occurring linguistic features" (Stubbs, 1997, p. 9), a key principle of MD analysis, rather than focusing solely on individual features. Although these suggestions may not have been embraced in the practice of CDA, they highlight the potential for applying MD principles to identify and critique ideological discourses from a corpus linguistic perspective. Essentially, these points lead to a multi-way characterization of texts and registers, away from binary distinctions. We argue that both suggestions can be incorporated in corpus-based analyses of discourse through LMDA, as we demonstrate in this Element.

In turn, CADS represents a development within corpus linguistics that integrates corpus-based methods and discourse analysis. Unlike CDA, where the integration of corpus methods was a subsequent development, CADS has incorporated corpus linguistics techniques as a fundamental part of its approach from its inception in the late 1990s and early 2000s. It emerged primarily in the UK and Italy through the pioneering work of researchers such as Paul Baker, Michael Stubbs, Tony McEnery, and Alan Partington. This development was facilitated by the increasing availability of both large corpora and personal corpus analysis software, such as WordSmith Tools (Scott, 1996).

As in corpus-assisted CDA, CADS researchers also rely on mainstream corpus tools such as concordances, keywords, and collocate and word lists, which enable them to both mine the corpus for the most salient linguistic features associated with a discursive issue and identify the patterns surrounding these linguistic features. As Gillings et al. (2023) put it, "corpus assistance helps us to link large-scale social phenomena with linguistic choices at the micro level." Analysts in CADS concentrate on uncovering recurrent patterns within the corpus, which is in line with the key concept of discursive repetition, "the idea that an attitude or ideology can be transmitted over a long period of time through people's repeated encounters with words or phrases, eventually resulting in a discourse being uncritically perceived as natural or normal" (Baker, in press).

Keyword analysis (Scott, 1996), which identifies words that are used statistically more frequently in one corpus compared to another, is a widely used method in CADS due to its utility in helping researchers sample a subset of words from the entire corpus that merit further investigation. Baker (2014) employed keyword analysis to investigate the gender differences hypothesis in language use, concluding that this hypothesis, as it pertains to lexical choice, was not substantiated by the data. Depending on how a keyword study is designed, the approach can be used to identify discourses or ideologies. For example, Baker and McEnery (2015) identified discourses about government benefits in a corpus of tweets by finding and grouping keywords.

In CADS, as in most keyword studies, the detection of keywords typically relies on frequency counts taken across the entire corpus rather than on a text-by-text basis (but see Egbert and Biber [2019] for a version of keyword analysis that uses text-based counts). This methodological choice can lead to skewed distributions of keyword usage. Such a skew arises because the corpus-wide counts may be influenced by the overuse of certain words by individual speakers or texts, rather than reflecting marked choices across the texts.

Collocational networks are an innovation aimed at flagging groups of collocations through visual displays that represent the connections among different individual collocations in a corpus. Tools like GraphColl, which is part of the LancsBox suite, provide capabilities for constructing collocation networks (i.e., associational relationships among a node's first and additional order collocates). A network is composed of different individual graphs, which can take various forms, including linear graphs, triangles, and quadrilaterals. As Baker (2016) shows, these different graphs can indicate specific linguistic patterns among the words, such as grammatical class membership, lexical bundles, or frames.

Each of these corpus linguistics approaches to discourse and ideologies is based on a theoretical relationship between lexical variables and ideological discursive constructs. The next subsection explores such theories.

1.5 Theories of Lexis

Though Stubbs (2015) indicates that there is no unified theory of lexis, most theoretical models that give prominence to lexis are rooted in collocation. These include theories of semantic prosody and semantic preference – and all variations in nomenclature referring to these ideas, extended lexical units (Stubbs, 2009), lexical priming (Hoey, 2005), and knowledge-free associative patterning (Phillips, 1985). A collocation is a node word and a word that repeatedly and meaningfully co-occurs with that node within a given local span in a text or a corpus. The local span is often four words to the left and four words to the right of the node. "Repeatedly" and "meaningfully" can be operationalized in a variety of ways by the analyst in terms of frequency and association (Brezina et al., 2015). Firth established the theoretical groundwork for collocation and famously claimed that we "shall know a word by the company it keeps" (1957/1968, p. 11). It has been well established that collocations can reveal socially loaded perspectives (Baker, 2010, 2016; Stubbs, 1996), and Baker (2016) shows how analysis of collocational networks can reveal information which may have "ideological significance" (p. 148).

Semantic preference and semantic prosody are two of the primary mechanisms through which collocation creates meaning. Semantic preference is also called semantic association (Hoey, 2005) and generally refers to the lexical set (i.e., thematic set) to which collocates of a node belong (e.g., the domain of medicine or the absence/change of state; Partington, 2004). Semantic prosody has two meanings (Hunston, 2007). The more common meaning is the evaluative (positive or negative) association a node and its collocates convey.

Semantic prosody in this sense is also called discourse prosody (Stubbs, 2001) and evaluative prosody (Partington et al., 2013). Hunston (2007) concludes that meaning derived from semantic preference and semantic prosody can often (but not always) be carried across texts by individual words. Finally, both semantic prosodies and semantic preferences are thought to often demonstrate register association (Partington, 2004).

Hoey's (2005) theory of lexical priming attempts to account for collocation observed in corpora through a psychological process of priming which is also sensitive to register. In this theory, at the local level, based on an individual's language experience, individual words are primed for collocation, semantic association (semantic preference), colligation, and pragmatic functions. Through a nesting operation, multi-word units are created with their own primes. At the level of text, words/multi-word units are primed to co-occur with other words/multi-word units in a text (textual collocation), in particular discourse functions (textual semantic association) and in particular sections of a text (textual colligation). In sum, the theory of lexical priming suggests that a large part of an individual's language can be accounted for through bottom-up processes driven by associational patterns in the lexical system with the text as an important unit of analysis.

Finally, Phillips (1985) hypothesizes that "a distributional analysis of linguistic substance; invoking no knowledge of the semantic content, the syntactic organization, or the lexical meaning of the text; would reveal global patternings in the lexis of the text" (p. 11) that he calls macrostructures. He goes on to test this hypothesis in a textbook, identifying the "aboutness" of chapters and the text as a whole based on frequency and associational measures of collocations, resulting in multiple groups of words he calls "lexical sets." While the macrostructure in question in this study is aboutness, ideological discourses can be similarly categorized as macrostructures (Ellis, 2019).

These theories indicate quite a bit about identifying ideological discourses from lexis. First, examining lexis through corpora reveals socially shared primings, collocations, semantic prosodies, and semantic preferences. As repositories of socially shared language, corpora reveal shared lexical primings, which in turn add to the priming data for authentic users of the language captured in a corpus. Hoey (2005) notes that "priming leads to a speaker unintentionally reproducing some aspect of language, and that aspect, thereby reproduced, in turn primes the hearer" (p. 9). As mentioned earlier, according to Hoey (2005), priming can explain collocation and Partington (2004) describes how socially shared primes account for socially shared semantic preferences and semantic prosodies, which are part of the communicative competence of individual speakers. He also presents a model in which collocations, semantic preferences, and semantic prosodies are all derived from text and each other in increasing levels of abstraction (with semantic prosodies being the most abstract). That is, a collocation is identified in a text, a semantic preference is identified from a set of collocations, and a semantic prosody is identified from a set of semantic preferences.

Second, these theories suggest that information about many linguistic levels seems to be accessible from associations among lexical items when text is the unit of analysis. Hoey (2005) shows how it is possible that the lexical system encodes the grammatical system, concluding that "what we think of as grammar is the product of the accumulation of all of the lexical primings in an individual's lifetime" (p. 159). Phillips (1985) is able to identify textual macrostructures from such associations. The underlying associative structure and successful performance of contemporary large language models (e.g., ChatGPT) also empirically validate this claim. Finally, the fact that collocations, semantic preferences, and semantic prosodies are all sensitive to register means that contextual/situational/social information must also be encoded in lexical distribution.

Therefore, taken together, theories of discourse and ideology and lexis, as well as corpus linguistics approaches to ideological discourses discussed in the previous subsection, suggest that examining associational, co-occurrence patterns of lexis through corpora using text as the unit of analysis can reveal ideological discourses. As repositories of socially shared language, depending on the alignment between the design of a specific corpus and the discourses being identified, corpora are ideal data sources. Lexis seems to be the appropriate linguistic level for identifying macrostructures such as ideological discourses conveyed through evaluative language. Partington's (2004) model sets up discourses as being an additional level of abstraction beyond semantic prosodies which can thus be derived from lexical co-occurrence. There is an indication that co-occurring sets of lexical items within and across texts carry ideological information. Finally, register seems to be an important delimiter in terms of both lexical association patterns and ideological expression, or, as Silverstein (1998, p. 126) puts it, "if all cultural and linguistic phenomena are essentially event linked, even where they appear to be manifestations of people's 'intuitions,' they are, as it were, ideological 'all the way down.'"

1.6 Similarities and Differences between Traditional and Lexical MDA

As LMDA is an extension of TMDA and both approaches have roots in the Flagstaff School of Corpus Linguistics (cf. Cortes & Csomay, 2015), their procedures are roughly the same and they share foundational assumptions. That is, as with conducting a TMDA, to conduct an LMDA, a researcher (1) constructs a corpus, (2) identifies variables for analysis, (3) counts occurrences of the variables per text, (4) subjects the counts to a multidimensional analysis to identify underlying constructs, and (5) for each dimension in the result, engages in qualitative analysis of texts with high values to interpret the underlying construct based on how the variables are deployed. However, distinct characteristics emerge as each approach is tailored to specific research goals. These differences and similarities will now be outlined, beginning with the common traits.

Variation: Both TMDA and LMDA are founded on the principle that language use inherently varies depending on the context. This means that language cannot be treated as a homogeneous entity; rather, its usage is shaped by the specific historical and contextual factors in which it occurs. Consequently, linguistic descriptions within these frameworks must account for systematic variation in language use.

Comprehensiveness: Both TMDA and LMDA assume a comprehensive approach to linguistic description, as opposed to a reductionist one. This means that their descriptions are based on a varied set of linguistic features, rather than starting off with just a few elements. This comprehensive approach allows for a more detailed and inclusive analysis of language use.

Co-occurrence: The need for a large and varied pool of linguistic features arises from the need to model linguistic co-occurrence; in turn, the relevance of co-occurrence arises from the fact that it reflects shared function (a communicative function for TMDA and a discursive function for LMDA). Since linguistic co-occurrence plays such a central role in MD analysis, it has achieved "formal status in the Multi-Dimensional approach to register variation" (Biber, 1995, p. 30).

Dimensionality: Both TMDA and LMDA share the hypothesis that latent constructs underlie language usage, shaped by the conditions in which language is used in natural settings. This hypothesis posits that these underlying constructs manifest as "dimensions" – sets of co-occurring linguistic features across texts.

Multidimensionality: Given that language variation is patterned by dimensions, and that multiple dimensions are needed to account for variation, both approaches are inherently multidimensional. This means they presuppose the simultaneous action of various dimensions on texts, shaping them to perform specific communicative functions in TMDA or to convey particular discourses or ideological formations in LMDA.

Parsimony: While both TMDA and LMDA utilize a large and varied set of linguistic features, their objective is to identify the smallest number of dimensions that account for language variation. This approach reduces the extensive initial set of individual characteristics into a few cohesive groups of variables, collectively explaining the variation observed across texts.

Comparative stance: Both TMDA and LMDA foster comparisons, as they highlight similarities and differences between various language varieties (TMDA) or social contexts (LMDA). By comparing different categories along the dimensions in extended study design, these categories can be more sharply portrayed.

Statistical foundation: Since a reliance on statistical methods is a defining trait of the Flagstaff School of Corpus Linguistics, both types of MD analysis depend on statistical analysis. These methods are essential for detecting latent phenomena, that is, constructs that while predicted are not directly observable. The primary statistical procedure in MD analysis is correlation, which is used to measure the systematic co-variation of variables. Given the comprehensive approach to the array of linguistic features and the goal of identifying dimensions of variation, MD analysis employs multivariate statistical techniques, including dimensionality reduction methods like factor analysis. The factors identified in such analyses represent sets of correlated variables, corresponding to patterns of cross-text variation.

Qualitative interpretation: Despite their strong quantitative foundation, both approaches necessitate qualitative interpretation of texts to assist in unveiling the underlying communicative functions (TMDA) or discourses (LMDA). Without careful interpretation, based on the consultation of numerous text samples, dimensions cannot emerge from factors.

Despite their similarities, TMDA and LMDA can be distinguished based on differing research goals, feature sets, and interpretive foci.

Research goals: TMDA is particularly relevant for research goals that focus on the functional aspects of language. This approach is grounded in the idea that shared linguistic features indicate a shared function. It is typically employed to describe register variation along functional lines, essentially detailing the differences and similarities across various registers in a language or domain. If a researcher's objective involves analyzing texts from a functional perspective through structural, syntactic, or morphological classes, then TMDA is the appropriate method.

In contrast, as presented in this Element, LMDA is designed to cater for the identification of latent, macro-level constructs encoded in discourse. The range of research goals that can be addressed with a focus on discourse is vast, covering such aspects as ideologies, representations, identities, themes, motifs, schemas, and many other conceptual systems. Thus, if the research goal includes describing the lexical materialization of such discourse-based constructs, then LMDA is the necessary method over TMDA.

Linguistic features: The features typically used in a TMDA are lexico-grammatical, comprising structural, syntactic, and morphological classes. The exact features to be used in a TMDA project depends on previous consideration of the features of relevance for the specific research goals. On the other hand, LMDA utilizes the actual words in the texts as its primary units of analysis, contrasting with the broader lexico-grammatical classes employed in TMDA. Thus, in an LMDA, the features used are entirely lexical, including the actual words, their base forms (lemmas), semantic categories, collocations, or n-grams.

Interpretive focus: TMDA primarily focuses on identifying functional parameters of variation in language. By "function," we refer to the communicative roles that linguistic features play, enabling users to perform specific tasks with language. As Biber and Conrad (2019, p. 2) state:

> The underlying assumption of the register perspective is that core linguistic features (e.g., pronouns and verbs) serve communicative functions. As a result, some linguistic features are common in a register because they are functionally adapted to the communicative purposes and situational context of texts from that register.

The dimensions in TMDA, which are correlated sets of linguistic features, correspond to the underlying macro communicative function of the texts. Researchers determine these underlying macro functions through factor interpretation, linking the linguistic patterns to the situational characteristics of the registers. Consequently, a functional interpretation of the patterns within these dimensions is essentially "an account of *why* these patterns exist" (Biber & Conrad, 2019, p. 69; emphasis in the original text).

Conversely, in LMDA, the interpretive focus is on unearthing the latent discourse constructs materialized in the texts. The interpretation taps into the potential of lexical features as signposts or entry points to the analysis of discourse, as acknowledged in corpus-assisted approaches to discourse analysis. For instance, according to Stubbs, lexical keywords are "nodes around which ideological battles are fought" (Stubbs, 2001, p. 188). Similarly, Mautner describes a word such as *entrepreneurship* as a "carrier of key values" (Mautner, 2005, p. 96), providing "focal points around which current discourses … crystallize" (Mautner, 2005, p. 111), in the context of educational entrepreneurialism. In turn, Krieg-Planque (2010, p. 9) considers that particular lexical expressions, which she refers to as "formulas," have a dual role of both constructing and crystallizing political and social issues. Meanwhile, TMDA offers limited entry points to the discursive layers of language because of its goal of describing variation at the functional level of language use.

1.7 Overview of Element

This section has presented the foundation of LMDA for identification of ideological discourses, demonstrating that the approach is grounded in (1) procedures of TMDA and CADS and (2) theories of lexis and discourse studies. Following this introduction, in Section 2, the major studies to date using LMDA will be synthesized. The synthesis will address variation in design and constructs identified, as well as lessons learned both in terms of methodology and theoretical advances. This section will explicitly and robustly attend to the range of meaning systems encoded in lexis that are identifiable by application of LMDA.

In Section 3, step-by-step guidance on how to perform an LMDA will be provided. The major methodological steps will be presented and illustrated, including corpus design, part-of-speech tagging and lemmatization, feature selection and counting, statistical analysis, and the interpretation of the results from both a qualitative and a quantitative perspective.

In Section 4, Case Study 1 will demonstrate how LMDA can be used to detect discourses in social media, more specifically on the conservative platform GETTR. The analysis focuses on the discourses around climate change underlying thousands of messages challenging environmental activism.

In Section 5, Case Study 2 will showcase how this approach allows researchers to explore the distribution of the constructs identified in LMDA over time or over other variables using inferential statistics. This case study uses four ideological discourses about twenty-first-century migrant education in the US.

Finally, Section 6 will briefly summarize the major points presented, consider the potential of the approach, and explore some of its possible future developments.

2 Synthesizing Existing LMDA Scholarship

2.1 Introduction

This section will focus on the LMDA studies conducted thus far. First, early LMDA studies directly grown out of TMDA will be presented, followed by more recent LMDA studies which have identified latent discursive constructs, explored the distribution of such constructs, derived additional measures from the latent discursive construct data, or some combination of these outcomes (Table 1).

Table 1 Existing LMDA studies and research questions addressed.

LMDA Study Outcome	Authors	Year	Research Questions
Establish foundation	Biber	(1993a)	*Which clusters of collocations reflect similar underlying word senses?* (p. 532)
Establish foundation	Crossley and Lowerse	(2007)	*Can categorizations be obtained using a simple n-gram algorithm?* (p. 457)
Identify latent discursive constructs	Fitzsimmons-Doolan	(2014)	*What is the language ideology profile expressed in Arizona Department of Education (ADE) language policy texts?* (p. 62)
Explore distribution of latent discursive constructs	Fitzsimmons-Doolan	(2019)	*Is there variation in the language ideologies expressed in a corpus of institutional language policy texts attributable to language policy register?*
Identify latent discursive constructs; explore distribution of latent discursive constructs	Berber Sardinha	(2019)	*What are the linguistic forms of representation connected to nationalities that have circulated in discourse over time?* (p. 232)
Derive additional measures from latent discursive construct data	Berber Sardinha	(2020)	*What is the historical distribution of representations of the United States and Brazil formed around the use of the nationality adjectives American and Brazilian?* (p. 183)
Identify latent discursive constructs; explore distribution of latent discursive constructs; derive additional measures from latent discursive construct data	Berber Sardinha	(2021)	*(1) What are the major discourses of applied linguistics? (2) How do these discourses shift over time? (3) What historical periods can be discerned based on these discourse shifts?* (p. 302)

Identify latent discursive constructs; derive additional measures from latent discursive construct data	Kauffman and Berber Sardinha (2021)	1. What are the functional and lexical dimensions of variation in Machado's major works? 2. What relationships can we find between the lexical and functional dimensions of variation through a canonical correlation analysis? (p. 358)
Identify latent discursive constructs	Clarke, McEnery, and Brookes (2021)	Can keywords be grouped into dimensions which may, where relevant, aid analysts in discovering groups of texts which represent discourses that are linked to specific subregisters? (p. 146)
Derive additional measures from latent discursive construct data	Berber Sardinha (2022a)	What discourses are present in an academic journal over a given time period? What are the major historical eras of that journal based on co-existing discourses?
Explore distribution of latent discursive constructs	Clarke, Brookes, and McEnery (2022)	What is the potential for keyword co-occurrence to identify changing discourses over time?
Identify latent discursive constructs	Fitzsimmons-Doolan (2023)	Which ideological discourses about im/migration are present in a multi-register corpus of 21st century texts about US migrant education?
Identify latent discursive constructs	Clarke (2024)	How are climate change and global warming represented in pseudoscience webtexts?
Explore distribution of latent discursive constructs	Fitzsimmons-Doolan This volume	What patterns related to register and time are apparent in the distribution of four ideological discourses about migrant education?

Next, cross-cutting patterns across this body of studies will be discussed, including variation in design and constructs identified, as well as lessons learned both in terms of methodology and theoretical advances. Though the identification of ideological discourses through LMDA are the focus of this Element, this synthesis will attend to the range of meaning systems encoded in lexis that have been identified through the application of LMDA.

2.2 Establishing a Foundation

As noted in Section 1, LMDA is an outgrowth of the methodological approach of TMDA, pioneered by Biber (Biber, 1988; Berber Sardinha & Veirano Pinto, 2019). Prior to the recent body of LMDA scholarship, two early studies, firmly grounded in the lexico-grammatical multidimensional analysis tradition, experimented with lexical variables. In a 1993 case study, Biber asked "which clusters of collocations reflect similar underlying senses" (Biber, 1993a, p. 532) in order to address gaps in lexicography methods at the time. Two nodes were used in the case study: *certain* and *right*. From a subsample of the Longman/Lancaster corpus, collocates occurring with each node more than thirty times were identified and the frequency counts of each collocation per text were computed and used in a factor analysis. The resulting factors were interpreted as word senses. For example, for the node, *right*, Factor 1 was directional (e.g., *right hemisphere*, *right side*) and Factor 2 conveyed immediacy (e.g., *right there*, *right now*). Later, addressing gaps from computational linguistics, Crossley and Louwerse (2007) used frequency counts of bigrams across multiple spoken and written corpora representing different registers in a factor analysis. The factors were interpreted as register dimensions (i.e., *scripted* vs. *unscripted*, *spatial* vs. *nonspatial*) and mean factor scores for each register were plotted to show how the registers differed for each factor/dimension of register variation. Both studies were interpreted as successful in addressing the subfield gaps they set out to address and laid the groundwork for future LMDA studies.

2.3 Identifying Latent Discursive Constructs

The primary outcome of an LMDA is the identification of a latent macrostructure encoded in lexis that conveys meaning. Such constructs include language ideologies, representations, discourses (both thematic and ideological), and thematic dimensions of literary style. Studies with this outcome are presented in the text that follows.

Fitzsimmons-Doolan (2014) used LMDA to identify and describe language ideologies. Modifier collocates (e.g., **academic** *language*, **adolescent** *literacy*, **ordinary** *English*) of node words representing language constructs (i.e., *academic **language**, adolescent **literacy**, ordinary **English***) were identified. A factor analysis was conducted using normed counts of occurrences of the collocates per text. The corpus under investigation contained language policy texts from the Arizona Department of Education (DOE) website. The resulting five factors indicated by co-occurring collocates were interpreted as language ideologies. For example, after investigating how they were deployed in texts, the co-occurring collocates on Factor 2 (i.e., *discrete, controversial, English, classroom, structured*) were interpreted as indexing the language ideology, *language acquisition is systematically metalinguistic and monolingual.*

Berber Sardinha and his associates have engaged in many LMDA studies to identify a variety of discourse constructs. Berber Sardinha (2019) applied LMDA to identify national representations. For two separate analyses, frequency counts per year of the bigrams AMERICAN + NOUN and BRAZILIAN + NOUN in the Google bigram database derived from Google Books from 1800–2008 were subjected to a factor analysis. The resulting five factors for each nationality were interpreted as national representations. For example, *superpower* vs. *local status* was identified as an American representation and *raw materials and the landscape* was identified as a Brazilian representation. Berber Sardinha (2021) reports multiple LMDA analyses concerned with identifying discourses in the discipline of applied linguistics over time. In the first analysis, normed counts of the most frequent noun, verb, and adjective lemmas per text in five applied linguistics journals over time were subjected to a factor analysis. This resulted in six discourses of applied linguistics (e.g., *applied linguistics as an empirical/physical/natural science, speech as interaction* vs. *speech as pronunciation*). A second LMDA in Berber Sardinha (2021) used the same variables/measures as the first analysis from research articles in *TESOL Quarterly* only and found five discourses (e.g., *linguistic theory* vs. *education*). In Kauffmann and Berber Sardinha (2021), an LMDA of a corpus of the works of Brazilian author, Machado de Assis, was conducted. Normed counts of 346 lemmas that met dispersion and frequency criteria were included in a factor analysis which resulted in nine factors interpreted as stylistic dimensions. These dimensions identified major themes in the author's work (e.g., *romance, love,* and *passion*).

Developing the approach of selecting lexical variables in relation to a node word, Fitzsimmons-Doolan (2023) applied LMDA to identify ideological discourses about migrant education. Using a multi-register corpus of twenty-first-century texts on the topic of migrant education developed for the study, 114 collocates (e.g., *services, reform, data,* and *law*) of the node *MIGR* that occurred in evaluating or modifying grammatical roles were identified as variables for the LMDA. Normed counts of the variables per text were used in a factor analysis and, after qualitative analysis focusing on the texts with the highest factor scores for each ideological discourse, the factors of co-occurring collocates were interpreted as ideological discourses (e.g., *US immigration policies are problematic, but there is no consensus for solutions*).

Finally, Clarke and her associates have recently engaged in a series of studies using multiple correspondence analysis (MCA) that identify patterns of variation in the co-occurrence of lexical variables. This approach, which the authors call keyword co-occurrence, first identifies keywords in a corpus of interest and then applies MCA to identify dimensions that are interpreted as representational discourses (Clarke, 2024; Clarke et al., 2021; Clarke et al., 2022).

2.4 Exploring Distribution of Latent Discursive Constructs

Once the latent discursive constructs have been identified, their distribution in the corpus according to another variable can be described. The most common variables by which the distribution has been studied are time and register. In a follow-up study to Fitzsimmons-Doolan (2014), Fitzsimmons-Doolan (2019) explored the distribution of the 2014 language ideologies across the corpus of policy webtexts by language policy register. After coding each text in the corpus by language policy register (see Lo Bianco, 2008) (i.e., language policy documents, discourse about language policy, institutional models of language policy, and lists), mean factor scores per register were used in analyses of variance for each language ideology. The analysis found that for four out of five language ideologies there were significant differences among language policy registers and that institutional models of language policy did "the ideological heavy lifting." Similarly, in Berber Sardinha (2019), which identified national representations in the Google Books corpus, for each representation, ANOVAs revealed significant and large differences in the distribution of the national representations between decades. In a follow-up study of their MCA of keywords from UK news texts about Islam, Clarke et al. (2022) plotted coordinates (measures of strength of discourse representation) for each article for each discourse to track representation of the discourse in the corpus over time.

Two studies have examined the distribution of discourses across multiple variables. In Berber Sardinha's (2021) study of discourses in applied linguistics journals, for each discourse, ANOVAs and coefficients of determination revealed significant effects for decade and journal as well as interaction effects. Finally, Section 5 in this Element presents a follow-up study in which a series of analyses of variance revealed how and to what degree four of the eleven ideological discourses identified in Fitzsimmons-Doolan (2023) varied over time (2003–17) and register (i.e., regional newspapers, national newspapers, newspaper comments, state DOE webtexts, federal DOE webtexts).

2.5 Deriving Additional Measures from the Latent Discursive Construct Data

Another outcome of LMDAs is the generation of information about additional variables using the latent discursive construct data as a source. For example, Berber Sardinha (2020) used factor scores for each year from the 2019 study of national representations in a cluster analysis to reveal historical periods for each nationality based on bigram co-occurrence patterns across dimensions. The analysis found eight historical clusters in the BRAZILIAN data ranging from *Cluster 1 – The 19th century: natural features and aspects of life* to *Cluster 8 – The late 20th and early 21st centuries: the economy, politics, arts, sciences, the people, religion and the environment.* Similarly, in Berber Sardinha's (2021) study of discourses in applied linguistic journals, a cluster analysis of factor scores revealed two historical eras across discourses: 1946–late 1980s and from the late 1980s to 2015. Berber Sardinha (2022a) extended the analysis of the LMDA of the TQ articles presented in the 2021 study by conducting a cluster analysis to identify major eras in the publication history of TQ based on the discursive variables. The cluster analysis identified two major eras: 1967–92 and 1993–2016.

Finally, Kauffmann and Berber Sardinha's (2021) study of Machado's literary texts helped make clear the wide range of research questions LMDA can be used to address. In addition to the LMDA reported earlier, a TMDA as well as canonical correlation analysis were applied to the corpus. The goal was to present an MDA-informed analysis of Machado's literary style. The TMDA used twenty-nine linguistic features related to style and identified five factors interpreted as functional and aesthetic dimensions of style (e.g., *narrative discourse*). A canonical correlation analysis merged the two MDAs and found four correlations (e.g., *introspective, formal romantic discourse*).

2.6 Looking Forward

Three additional unpublished studies across different domains demonstrate additional possibilities for LMDA outcomes. In Berber Sardinha (2023), the discourses surrounding the COVID-19 pandemic were analyzed using a 825-million-word sample from the Coronavirus corpus (Davies, 2021). In this study, four lexical dimensions were identified, each corresponding to a significant representation of the pandemic from its onset in 2020 up to March 2021. The study demonstrated the scalability of LMDA for larger corpora. In Berber Sardinha (2024), a curated corpus of messages and images posted on Twitter by climate action supporters and deniers of human-led climate change was employed to detect the major discourses shaping the online debate on this issue. A key methodological innovation was the application of LMDA to detect visual dimensions based on the automatic annotation of social media images using computer vision technology. Finally, Berber Sardinha et al. (2022) used a similar design to Kauffmann and Berber Sardinha (2021) and merged semantic dimensions from an LMDA of song lyrics and acoustic dimensions from a second MDA of Spotify acoustic tags on the same songs in a canonical correlation analysis.

Taken together, among these seventeen studies using LMDA techniques, a number of cross-cutting patterns emerge. These are addressed in the next subsections.

2.7 Inputs Change the Outputs

While the basic technique in LMDA remains constant, there are several deliberate design permutations across the fifteen published LMDA studies that change the analysis results. That is, all LMDA studies use measures of lexical variables across a corpus of texts in a multidimensional (usually factor) analysis to identify co-occurrence patterns among the variables. However, when different lexical variables are used or a different unit of measure is used, different constructs are identified through the factor analysis. Table 2 presents the fifteen published LMDA studies grouped into sets by similar designs, as well as the lexical variable, variable measure, and the construct operationalized from the resulting factors for each study.

Design Sets 1–2 used associated word pairs (e.g., collocates, bigrams) as the lexical variable. Both Biber (1993a) and Crossley and Louwerse (2007) counted associated word pairs per text, but because Biber's collocations all had the same node, while Crossley and Louwerse's bigrams had no shared lexical item, the constructs identified were unrelated (words senses [semantic] vs. dimensions of register variation [functional]). Berber Sardinha (2019, 2020) used bigrams as the lexical variable, but each bigram had the same node (i.e., AMERICAN or BRAZILIAN) and the location (R1) and word class (noun) of the associated lexical item was specified. Therefore, the identified construct was national representation.

The remaining studies (Design Sets 3–6) used single lexical units as the variables. The Fitzsimmons-Doolan studies all used counts/text of collocates of a node. The collocates were specified by a modifying or evaluative grammatical function, which supported the identification of ideological constructs (i.e., language ideologies, ideological discourses). The next set of studies use lemmas identified by frequency and dispersion criteria. Berber Sardinha (2021) and (2022a) included only lemmas tagged as nouns, adjectives, or verbs. These

Table 2 Published LMDA studies grouped by similar design characteristics.

Design Set	Study	Lexical Variable	Measure	Construct Identified
1	Biber (1993a)	Collocation	Frequency/text	Word senses
	Crossley and Louwerse (2007)	Bigrams	Frequency/text	Dimensions of register variation
2	Berber Sardinha (2019, 2020)	National adj + noun bigrams	Normed frequency/year	National representations
3	Fitzsimmons-Doolan (2014, 2019)	Modifier collocates	Normed frequency/text	Language ideologies
	Fitzsimmons-Doolan (2023, this volume)	Modifier collocates (extended set)	Normed frequency/text	Ideological discourses
4	Berber Sardinha (2021)	Noun, adj, verb lemmas	Normed frequency/year	Discourses
	Berber Sardinha (2022a)	Noun, adj, verb lemmas	Normed frequency/year	Discourses
	Kauffmann and Berber Sardinha (2021)	Lemmas	Normed frequency/text	Thematic dimensions of literary style
5	Berber Sardinha (this volume)	Lemmas	Presence or absence/text	Discourses
6	Clarke, McEnery, and Brookes (2021); Clarke, Brookes, and McEnery (2022); and Clarke (2024)	Keywords	Presence or absence of keyword/text	Discourses

resulted in the identification of discourses that were thematic in nature. Kauffmann and Berber Sardinha (2021) also used lemmas as the lexical variable, but because of the design of the corpus (all texts were written by the same author), the analysis resulted in the identification of dimensions of style specific to that author. In the case study presented in this Element, Berber Sardinha took into account the occurrence or nonoccurrence of content word lemmas to identify discourses in social media posts. Finally, the studies by Clarke used counts of the presence or absence of keywords per text which resulted in dimensions interpreted as discourses. Thus, LMDA offers a framework for identifying latent constructs conveyed through lexis. However, the LMDA framework has several points of design flexibility (i.e, variable selection, measure selection, and corpus design) that allow for nuance in the construct identified.

2.8 Broad Topical Application and Extension

In addition to the variety of lexically driven constructs that can be studied using the approach, this review of LMDA studies reveals a broad range of academic fields informed by these analyses. These include computational linguistics, discourse studies, historiography, language policy, lexicography, literary stylistics, music psychology, public health, public science, and register studies. This breadth suggests that as the approach becomes more developed and specified, interdisciplinary collaboration between corpus linguists and scholars from a host of academic fields should be productive.

Furthermore, across the current batch of LMDA studies, there is a clear pattern of analytical extension. That is, each of the more recent LMDA studies involves additional statistical analysis beyond the initial factor analysis. Four analysis types have been used for this extension. Once the LMDA has identified the latent lexically driven constructs, analyses of variance (e.g., ANOVAs) can be run to determine whether independent variables such as time, register, or source have a significant effect on the identified constructs (Berber Sardinha, 2019, 2020, 2021; Fitzsimmons-Doolan, 2019, this volume). Provided the factor analysis has identified interdependent factors, cluster analysis can also be used with an independent variable (e.g., year) to identify aggregated units of that variable (e.g., historical era) informed by correlations among the factors/constructs with respect to the independent variable (Berber Sardinha, 2020, 2021, 2022a). If an LMDA has been conducted in addition to another MDA (e.g., TMDA or another LMDA), a canonical correlation analysis can merge the two

Lexical Multidimensional Analysis

MDAs to identify composite constructs (Berber Sardinha et al., 2022; Kauffmann & Berber Sardinha, 2021). This extension can be used to conduct multimodal analysis (e.g., Berber Sardinha, 2024). These extension analyses are possible because LMDA assigns quantitative values to both the variables/construct and the observations (i.e., texts/construct). These values can then be input into the extension analyses. These analytical extensions represent an important contribution of LMDA as an approach to the study of constructs like discourse and ideology, which are usually identified through qualitative analysis that doesn't provide a standardized result output that can be carried over into subsequent analyses.

2.9 Methodological Considerations

At least two important methodological considerations become clear in the survey of existing LMDA studies. The first is how to address zero counts in the data. The frequency of occurrence of many lexical items in language is less than that of grammatical items due to the Zipfian distribution of lexis (Biber et al., 1998; Crossley et al., 2014). Therefore, unless adjustments are made, when lexical variables are used, especially in shorter texts, it is likely that the analyst will have an abundance of zero counts. Excessive zeros in datasets for factor analysis can be problematic (Keller et al., 2022; Xu et al., 2020). The preceding studies have addressed this issue in several ways. For example, Fitzsimmons-Doolan (2014) applied a *log transformation* ($\log 10\ X_i + 1$) to the normed counts of the data which reduced the number of zero counts and improved factorability. Crossley and Louwerse (2007) used *dispersion* criteria. That is, only bigrams that were present in each observed text were included in the analysis, which eliminated zero counts. *Frequency* was another approach which addressed this issue. Berber Sardinha (2022a) identified the most frequent lemmas in the data, which indirectly reduced the number of zero values. In fact, many of the studies applied some combination of the these approaches to handling the absence of lexical variables in observations (i.e., true zeros). Finally, Clarke et al. (2021) used multiple correspondence analysis (MCA) instead of a factor analysis in their keyword co-occurrence studies. In MCA, the presence or absence of a variable/observation is used as a measure rather than variable count/observation and it is thus not hamstrung by zero counts.

As in LMDA, in NLP the problem of zero-inflated datasets is a common issue. To avoid this sparsity problem, NLP researchers use word vectors or embeddings. Word vectorization is the process of converting text data to numerical vectors, projecting words to a low-dimensional space and positioning related words close together while keeping unrelated words far apart. Generally, word embeddings comprise between 200 and 300 dimensions, resulting in each word being represented by a sequence of 200 or 300 numbers, rather than by the counts of those words in the actual texts.

Another methodological consideration evident across the studies is how to interpret poles when the lexical LMDA results in dimensions with highly loading positive and negative lexical variables. For each dimension in a factor analysis or MCA result, each variable in the analysis is given a factor loading. To interpret the factors as constructs (e.g., discourses), the variables with positive loadings above an a priori cutoff threshold (e.g., 0.3) are investigated qualitatively in the corpus. In the LMDA analyses conducted thus far, the factors often only have variables with positive loadings. However, on occasion, the factors have variables with negative factor loadings that exceed the cutoff threshold and the meaning of these poles of the factor must be interpreted as well. In traditional MDA, poles are understood as complementary of one another (Biber et al., 1998). As Friginal and Hardy (2019) explain, "this distribution shows the relationship between two different groups of elements of the same kind, where one element is found in one set of environments and the other element is found in a nonintersecting (i.e., complementary) set of environments" (p. 147). In the LMDA studies, there is not consistency in how the negative poles are interpreted relative to the positive poles. Across the LMDA studies conducted thus far, approaches to interpreting factors with poles include labels that describe:

(1) opposites of a type (e.g., scripted vs. unscripted discourse; Crossley & Louwerse, 2007);
(2) differences of a type (e.g., speech as interaction vs. speech as pronunciation; Berber Sardinha, 2022a);
(3) different entities with no unifying connection (e.g., literate expression vs. revolution and the new nation; Berber Sardinha, 2019);
(4) one entity that accounts for complementary distribution (e.g., nativeness of skills mark group variation; Fitzsimmons-Doolan, 2014).

Future specification of LMDA, then, might endeavor to provide guidance for interpreting results when two poles are identified.

2.10 Patterns in Lexis Reveal Latent Systems of Meaning

Taken together, the LMDA studies affirm that a number of distinct latent meaning systems are created through repetition and co-occurrence of lexical items and point to important moderating variables. These meaning systems range from word senses (Biber, 1993a) to ideological discourses (Fitzsimmons-Doolan, 2023) to national representations (Berber Sardinha, 2019), and are identifiable through linguistic analysis as demonstrated through these studies. Furthermore, these latent meaning systems have social validity, as established by the interpretability of the factors. Many of the research questions addressed by these LMDA studies – especially those that pertain to ideological discourses – are usually explored using techniques outside of corpus linguistics (CL). Thus, the application of LMDA affords the benefits of CL analysis (large datasets, inductive analysis, analysis of full texts) to be applied to these domains of inquiry. Though CL techniques such as collocation and keyness analysis can be used in the study of discourses (e.g., Gabrielatos & Baker, 2008), LMDA extends the CL analysis farther into the process by grouping variables for interpretation, reducing (but not eliminating) subjectivity and increasing replicability. Moreover, a number of the LMDA studies addressed the issue of lexical distribution and register as a moderating variable either by testing related hypotheses (e.g., Crossley & Louwerse, 2007) or exploring the distribution of latent meaning systems by (Fitzsimmons-Doolan, 2019) or across register (Fitzsimmons-Doolan, 2023). This is perhaps not surprising given the focus on register in TMDA.

In addition, the LMDA approach, with its reliance on human interpretation of the texts where the statistical patterns are present, can yield insights that computational approaches with limited or no human interpretative engagement cannot. Computational approaches such as topic modeling, while proficient in processing large datasets and identifying statistical patterns, encounter significant limitations when tasked with revealing discourses because such approaches that rely on limited human text interpretation are restricted to surface-level patterns, whereas a focus on discourses requires consideration of historical, social, and political contexts, which are not immediately noticeable at the surface. For instance, the factor pattern for Dimension 2 from the first case study presented in this Element includes such lemmas as *temperature, earth, scientist, warm, weather, warming, dioxide, atmosphere, decade, hot, ice,* and *age*, which at the surface could be interpreted as indexing "global warming" discourse; however, by interpreting the actual texts where these items occur, it is possible to discern a more specific discourse that frames global warming as a form of alarmism promoted by climate activists. The positive pole of the dimension was therefore labeled as "activism alarmism" to reflect this underlying discourse.

2.11 Conclusion

In sum, the current body of scholarship using LMDA demonstrates that LMDA offers a versatile and broadly insightful method for analyzing large bodies of linguistic data to identify covert discursive and ideological meaning systems. In addition to modifications in corpus design, the lexical variables and their measures can be manipulated to identify a range of latent constructs. Moreover, LMDA can be applied to address research questions across a variety of academic fields of inquiry. Finally, in an age where the rate and scope of linguistic communication is unprecedented, LMDA can both identify and provide critical behavioral information about meaning systems harbored in language which are serving as catalysts for rapid social change.

3 How to Conduct a Lexical Multidimensional Analysis

In this section, we offer practical assistance with the technical aspects of LMDA, primarily focusing on conducting LMDA within a programming interface paired with statistical software. However, it is also possible to conduct the analysis using corpus software such as WordSmith (Scott, 2016) and statistical software. Notes on the latter approach are provided throughout as well.

3.1 A Note on Corpus Design

Corpus design plays a crucial role in MDA, serving as the foundation for meaningful results. Due to space constraints in this Element, a comprehensive overview of corpus design is not possible here. Detailed discussions on this topic, including the critical aspect of corpus representativeness, can be found elsewhere (Biber, 1993b; Egbert, 2019; Egbert et al., 2022; Berber Sardinha (to appear)).

This brief overview will only highlight the importance of text centrality in the construction of corpora for LMDA studies, where the emphasis is on treating each text as an individual observation unit. Essentially, MDA is a text analytical approach, centering on the analysis of text collections; as such, the text is the unit of observation. This is in contrast with other corpus linguistic approaches where the corpus itself is the unit of observation. In MD studies, statistics are conducted based on the count of texts where the variables occur, rather than the count of the variables across the whole corpus (Gray, 2013).

In a corpus tailored for MDA, where texts are treated as the observation unit, each file should comprise a single full text. Metadata are often added to the corpus, containing information about each text detailing the context (e.g., register, source, date, etc.). In corpora not designed around individual texts as observation units, files might contain several texts or only text fragments, and metadata for each text may not be provided.

Because of the central role played by texts in an MD corpus, researchers must take into consideration how many texts will be collected and how they will be distributed across the corpus categories (registers, domains, time periods, publishers, social media platforms or users, etc.). The general goal is to collect representative samples for the different corpus categories (Biber, 1993b; Egbert, 2019; Egbert et al., 2022; Berber Sardinha (to appear)). According to Egbert et al. (2022), corpus representativeness can be understood as the extent to which a corpus enables researchers to make generalizations about the typical quantitative linguistic patterns found in a particular language or domain. As achieving representativeness is a complex undertaking, a thorough discussion is not within the scope of this Element; readers are encouraged to refer to Egbert, Biber, and Gray (2022), Biber (1993b), and Berber Sardinha (to appear) for a fuller treatment.

Considerations of corpus size form an integral part of the design criteria, which should be guided by the goal of ensuring representativeness. Typically, MD corpora are not designed to meet a particular word count total because, as mentioned, the unit of observation in MD corpus design is not the word, but the text. When determining the number of texts to include in a corpus, the guiding principle should be representativeness rather than an arbitrary figure. However, the requirements of statistical procedures such as factor analysis regarding dataset size must be taken into account. Factor analysis requires that the number of observations (texts) surpasses the number of variables (linguistic features) involved. Typically, it is advisable to have a ratio of at least five observations for every variable in factor analysis (Gorsuch, 2015). Based on this guideline, an LMDA study involving 500 lexical variables should aim for a minimum corpus size of 2,500 texts.

3.2 Corpus Processing

The following steps outline the procedures for corpus processing, essential for conducting an LMDA. Detailed descriptions of these steps and additional guidelines, together with computer code, are provided in the online appendix, available for further reference.

1. Lemmatization and part-of-speech tagging: If the lexical variable in the study is a lemma, all words within the corpus undergo lemmatization and are tagged for their part of speech. This step standardizes the text and facilitates subsequent analysis.

2. Frequency, keyness, and dispersion: The next step involves calculating the frequency, keyness, or dispersion of the lexical variables (or "features," in MDA terminology).
3. Selection of features of interest: After the features have been quantified, specific words or sets of words are selected based on their relevance to the research objectives. For instance, one might focus on all nouns, words modifying particular nouns, or words that meet specific thresholds of frequency, keyness, and dispersion.
4. Factor analysis for identifying co-occurrence patterns: The selected features are then subjected to factor analysis, a statistical method used to identify sets of correlated words. Each factor is characterized by its loadings, which indicate the extent of co-occurrence among the words within the factor. The resulting factors are akin to those found in TMDA but consist of sets of words rather than grammatical features.

3.3 Factor Interpretation

Factor – or dimension – interpretation is an iterative and cyclical approach, where interpretive labels are proposed and refined to encapsulate the essence of the resulting factors. Interpretation begins by examining the lexical units that are highly loading on each factor to formulate initial hypotheses about the underlying discourses or ideologies. Analysts can initially draft temporary dimension labels based on the factor pattern, using the table listing the words loading on each factor. The next step involves consulting the texts themselves to test and refine these initial hypotheses. It is common for the analyst's initial impressions about the labels to evolve significantly as they progress through the interpretive process.

A critical part of factor interpretation includes considering the scores of the texts and, if applicable, how these scores are distributed among different corpus categories such as time period, register, or author. Analysts must interpret a large and varied selection of corpus texts to accurately discern the underlying discourses or ideologies. There is no fixed number of texts that must be consulted; the guiding principle is to review as many texts as necessary, particularly those with marked scores on a given pole, to solidify the descriptive labels. When the analyst considers that the descriptive labels are stable when confronted with more texts, then this usually means that the interpretation can be concluded.

The selection of texts for the interpretive analysis should be guided by two criteria: the factor score and (if available) the text category. Priority should be given to high-scoring texts from categories with the most extreme mean scores on the dimension under analysis. This ensures a focus on the most representative texts for each dimension.

Text interpretation should always be linked back to the overall discourse or ideology associated with the factor to avoid being sidetracked by the idiosyncrasies of individual texts and should pay attention to how the lexical variables are operating in the text. For those working in WordSmith, the variables of interest can all be highlighted for texts of interest, which aids this stage of the analysis. Analysts should strive to make explicit how the texts incorporate the discourse under consideration through the lexical items that load on the factor. As this is a process of constant fine-tuning, the descriptive labels for each factor are likely to undergo multiple iterations, evolving with increased insights from text consultation.

Furthermore, the interpretation process must be contextualized within the larger social and historical backdrop of the texts, considering aspects like the ideologies of the authors, the source, the time period, and political affiliations. Keeping in mind the concept of discourse formation, as described by Pecheux (1982, p. 111), can be helpful in this process:

> a discursive formation [is] that which in a given ideological formation ... determines 'what can and should be said ...' (Haroche et al., 1971, p. 102). This amounts to saying that words, expressions, propositions, etc., obtain their meaning from the discursive formation in which they are produced.

This concept can help analysts guide their interpretation by considering that the wording of the texts is constrained by the discursive formation (alternatively, "the things that are admitted within the discourse and the things that are omitted," according to Webster, 2003, p. 86), reminding them to make connections between the individual texts, the dimension, and the larger political context in which the text is embedded.

The interpretation must take into account the lexical items loading on each factor. Although the factor pattern is a decontextualized list of lexical items (e.g., lemmas), we do not base our interpretation on these lists. Rather, we emphasize the contextual interpretation of words within their specific textual environments marked by dimension scores. Rather than relying on isolated word lists, researchers must extensively analyze texts to determine the precise sense in which each lexical item is used. This involves careful examination of how each word functions within its surrounding linguistic context. We suggest that researchers select a sample of texts from the corpus to analyze each dimension (pole), which involves ranking the texts by their dimension score and selecting as many as feasible from the top-ranked texts for interpretation.

Although the lexical items loading on a factor may be polysemous, in our experience the polysemy is reduced because the range of senses for a word is constrained by the discourses underlying the dimension. We determine the word senses by analyzing texts marked for the specific dimensions where the lexical items appear. To illustrate, let us take Case Study 1 reported in this Element (Section 4), which focuses on conservative social media discourses challenging climate change. Dimension 2 from this study comprises polysemous words, such as *fire* and *toxic*. The lemma *fire* occurred in 97 out of 3,045 messages with a score of at least 2. Among these, ninetey-four instances (96.9 percent) referred to "material that is burning, producing flames, heat, and light, possibly with smoke," while three instances (3.1 percent) referred to "terminating someone from their job." Similarly, the lemma *toxic* appeared fifteen times, with ten instances (66.7 percent) meaning "poisonous" and five instances (33.3 percent) indicating "very unpleasant or unacceptable." When considering the top 300 highest scoring texts, all four instances referred to "poisonous." This suggests that higher dimension scores correlate with more restricted lemma senses, reflecting the underlying discourses indexed by the dimension. (All the word senses mentioned are from the Cambridge English Dictionary, https://dictionary.cambridge.org.)

Although dimension labels are typically concise, consisting of just a few words, accurately capturing the multifaceted nature of discourse sometimes necessitates longer, more descriptive labels. To address this, researchers may opt for a dual-labeling approach, employing both "longhand" and "shorthand" styles during interpretation. The longhand style offers a detailed description of the discourses or ideologies, capturing as much nuance as possible. Long labels may consist of an array of terms, as in Webster's (2003, p. 85) characterization of business discourse as "management-centered, ethically decontextualized, universalizing, libertarian, Darwinian, consumerist, and alarmist," or a whole sentence, as in "Immigrants and governments have a mutual relationship founded on acts of service and work" (see Case Study 2, Section 5), referring to discourses around migrant education.

In turn, the shorthand style provides a brief summary of the discourses, as "Discrediting climate change" (see Case Study 1, Section 4). Researchers can choose which style to use in their publications or presentations, depending on the level of detail and context required for their specific research output.

Experience shows that factor interpretation is often more effective when conducted in teams rather than individually. The collaborative approach mitigates potential bias by allowing different researchers to bring diverse perspectives and insights. (For more details on this interpretive process, see Fitzsimmons-Doolan, 2023, or Friginal and Hardy, 2019.)

To illustrate the process of factor interpretation, we refer to Dimension 2 of the first case study (see Section 4). This dimension comprises two complementary discourses, namely "Activism Alarmism vs. Progressive Measures Dismissal," each found on a different pole of the factor – the positive pole corresponds to *activism alarmism*, and the negative pole to *progressive measures dismissal*. For the purposes of this illustration, we will focus on the positive pole only, but a similar process was employed for the negative pole as well.

The first step in identifying the underlying discourses is to derive interpretive hypotheses based of the words with high loadings on Factor 2 (see Table 7). The terms that load heavily on this factor include *temperature, earth, scientist, warm, weather, warming, dioxide, atmosphere,* and *carbon,* among others. These terms are strongly associated with discussions around climate change, specifically the scientific and environmental aspects of the topic. Additionally, words like *lie, hoax, alarmist, fake,* and *narrative* signal a discourse of skepticism or outright rejection of mainstream climate science, often framing it as exaggerated or deceitful. The combination of scientific terminology with skeptical or pejorative language suggests a discourse that engages with the topic of climate change by casting doubt on its legitimacy and portraying it as a form of alarmism.

Once we have our initial hypothesis, we need to check it against the actual texts. It's useful not to select texts at random, but rather to select high-scoring texts and read them to confirm whether the hypothesized discourse patterns are indeed present and consistent across different examples. If these patterns are not present, we need to reconsider our initial interpretation, either by refining the hypothesis or by exploring alternative explanations for the observed word loadings. If the patterns are indeed present, then this provides support for the initial hypothesis, allowing us to proceed with labeling the dimension in a way that reflects the underlying discourse.

Here's an example text that scored 16 on this dimension pole by using these lemmas: *amazing, carbon, cause, climate, continued, decade, dioxide, global, heat, man, mongering, planet, rise, scientist, warm, warming,* and *year*:

> 5/x Scientists seeking funding and journalists seeking an audience agree: PANIC SELLS. Here's the continued list – an amazing chronology of the last 120 years of scare-mongering on climate • 1938 – Global warming, caused by man heating the planet with carbon dioxide, "is likely to prove beneficial to mankind in several ways, besides the provision of heat and power."– Quarterly Journal of the Royal Meteorological Society • 1938 – "Experts puzzle over 20 year mercury rise . . . Chicago is in the front rank of thousands

of cities throughout the world which have been affected by a mysterious trend toward warmer climate in the last two decades" – Chicago Tribune #ClimateScam . . .

The text mocks the historical predictions of climate change and presents them as examples of *scare-mongering*, which aligns with the initial hypothesis. At the same time, other discourses potentially present in the text may complicate this interpretation. This complexity is common in discourse analysis of corpus data, where different discourses often coexist and are meshed together in layers within the same text. It is important to keep track of these discourses and write down suitable labels to capture their essence. At this stage, the labels are temporary, serving as reminders of the discourses encountered in the texts.

One of these discourses present in the text is scientific skepticism. The text references scientists and journalists as complicit in promoting panic for personal gain (*Scientists seeking funding and journalists seeking an audience agree: PANIC SELLS*). This implies a skepticism not just toward climate change predictions, but more broadly toward the motivations and integrity of those who promote them. The phrase *PANIC SELLS* suggests that climate science is driven more by financial or career incentives than by genuine concern for the environment. This discourse shifts the focus from simply dismissing alarmist narratives to questioning the credibility and motivations of the scientific community. An underlying discourse of discrediting the scientific establishment seems to be present. Thus, we can add a label such as "scientific discrediting" to our provisional list of discourses.

We continue interpreting hundreds of texts and noting down the discourses that crop up. For example, text 5,843 (with a score of 14) claims that historical data contradicts the narrative of man-made climate change, describing it as a deliberate hoax. And text 5,783 (also with a score of 14) criticizes the evolution of climate-related discourse from global warming to climate change, suggesting that it is a catch-all term used to incite fear regardless of actual weather conditions. Incrementally, the discourse of "activism alarmism" emerges as a recurring theme, characterized by a systematic effort to portray climate activism as exaggerated, deceitful, and driven by ulterior motives.

Using the term *activism* to describe the discourse helps to reflect the target of the discourse – namely, the actions and rhetoric of climate advocates. The texts analyzed do not merely criticize scientific claims in isolation; they are specifically concerned with the way these claims are employed by a particular organized group to push for political and social change. The term *activism* underscores the focus on the political and social dimensions of the discourse, highlighting the perception that climate change action is not just about raising awareness but is seen as a forceful, sometimes manipulative, driver of alarmist narratives, spread for political gain.

As we interpret more and more texts, the label of *activism alarmism* persists as a viable descriptor as it becomes clear that these additional discourses do not stand alone; they are intertwined with and reinforce the overarching narrative of alarmism. The critique of scientific integrity and the portrayal of climate discourse as a manipulative tool are used to discredit climate change as a form of alarmism.

It is important to recognize that the process of interpreting texts to assign a dimension label is inherently subjective. However, this subjectivity must be mitigated by relying on corpus evidence, as is standard practice in corpus linguistics. This is part of a continuous process of refining hypotheses and established interpretations against more data and domain-specific information, in this case, climate change and conservative ideology. This iterative process helps ensure that the final dimension labels are well supported, capturing the complexities of the discourse while standing up to scrutiny.

4 Case Study 1: The Discourses Around Climate Change on a Conservative Social Media Platform

Tony Berber Sardinha

4.1 Introduction

In this section, we look at the application of LMDA to the identification of the discourses around climate change on the GETTR social media network. In mid 2021, GETTR was launched as a social media platform that caters primarily to right-wing followers, who see it as a forum for "free speech." Former US President Donald Trump has been closely associated with the founding of GETTR, as the platform was launched by Jason Miller, one of his former senior advisers. The platform was created in response to the banning of Trump from major platforms like Twitter and Facebook following the January 6, 2021, US Capitol riot.

Climate change advocacy or environmental activism, as a significant global movement, began to take shape in the late twentieth century, though its roots can be traced back to earlier environmental concerns. The modern movement gained substantial momentum following the establishment of the United

Nations Framework Convention on Climate Change (UNFCCC) in 1992 and the subsequent Kyoto Protocol in 1997.

The ideological core of climate change advocacy revolves around several key points, such as the acknowledgment of climate change as a critical and urgent global issue, the recognition of human activity, particularly the burning of fossil fuels, as a primary driver of climate change, and the imperative for immediate and coordinated global action to mitigate and adapt to its effects. This advocacy emphasizes transitioning to renewable energy sources, reducing carbon emissions, and protecting and restoring ecosystems.

The US conservative political movement combats pro-climate action because it often perceives the proposed environmental policies and regulations as threats to economic growth, personal freedoms, and national sovereignty. Many conservatives argue that the changes advocated by climate activists could lead to increased government intervention in the economy, potentially harming industries, particularly those in the fossil fuel sector, and resulting in job losses. There is also a concern that the costs associated with transitioning to a greener economy could burden taxpayers and consumers without guaranteeing significant environmental benefits. Additionally, some conservatives contend that climate change advocacy in the US is influenced by foreign interests (foremost from China) aiming to weaken the US economy.

While many conservatives acknowledge the rise in the Earth's temperatures, they dispute the assertion that human activity is the primary driver of this warming. Consequently, a central tenet of their ideology is the rejection of anthropogenic global warming (AGW), contradicting the widely accepted scientific view that human-induced factors, such as greenhouse gas emissions, are significantly contributing to climate change. Instead, they often propose an alternative hypothesis: that the observed warming is a result of the Earth's natural climatic cycles. This viewpoint suggests that the current changes in global temperatures are part of a normal, historical pattern of climatic variability, independent of human influence.

Climate change skepticism relies on a coordinated public discourse to confront the widely accepted scientific understanding of climate change and influence public opinion and policy. Platforms like GETTR are instrumental in this process, creating a robust community of skeptics who validate, legitimize, and normalize their ideology.

The effectiveness of coordinated anti-climate action discourse can be measured by the decline in American belief in the existence of climate change. As noted by Hoffmann (2011), between 2008 and 2009, belief among Americans dropped from 71 percent to 57 percent, and as of recent measurements, it stands at 54 percent (despite a wide split along party lines and age groups), suggesting that climate change skepticism is becoming increasingly normalized.

4.2 Methodology

The corpus used for this case study was designed to represent social media conversations about climate change from a conservative perspective. The composition of the corpus is displayed in Table 3. The corpus comprises posts written in English (either exclusively or alongside an additional language) that include at least one of these terms: *climate change*, *global warming*, *ESG* (environmental, social, and governance), *anthropogenic*, or *AGW* (anthropogenic global warming).

The posts were automatically collected using the *gogettr* Python scraping tool. Subsequently, they underwent processing via a script developed by the author, which executed tasks such as corpus cleaning and formatting. This included removing duplicate posts and converting emoji characters. The emoji conversion utilized a modified version of the demoji Python library, transforming each emoji into a standardized text label. Table 4 illustrates this process: The first sample shows the original post, followed by its processed version. In the processed version, emojis were converted into a label denoted by *EMOJI*, web links were removed and replaced with *URL*, usernames were anonymized with a generic label, and tokenization was applied by inserting a space before punctuation marks.

Each post was then tagged for part of speech with the TreeTagger (Schmid, 1994), which enabled the retrieval of the content words in each post, namely nouns, adjectives, verbs, and adverbs. The lemmas of the word tagged for each of these parts of speech were extracted using a purpose-built script.

In very short texts such as social media posts, the relative counts of the lexical features are unstable, that is, they are subject to large shifts caused by a single word or phrase due to the limited overall word count. In the current study, to circumvent the instability of feature counts, the lemma counts were converted to

Table 3 Climate change GETTR corpus (CCGC).

Year	Texts	Words	Mean Text Length	Text Length SD
2021	63	1,278	20.3	16.2
2022	1,853	40,433	21.8	17.3
2023	3,193	79,529	25.9	18.9
Total	5,109	121,240	23.7	18.3

Table 4 Original and processed versions of the same post.

Version	Post
Original	DR. CAL BEISNER – THE PUSH FOR GAS STOVE BANS But folks who are terrified about so-called catastrophic anthropogenic global warming want us to stop using gas @aubreysamerica 🚨 SUBSCRIBE TO OUR SUBSTACK: https://realamericasvoice.substack.com/subscribe 🔥 GET YOUR RAV GEAR: https://realamericasvoice.launchcart.store/
Processed	DR. CAL BEISNER – THE PUSH FOR GAS STOVE BANS But folks who are terrified about so-called catastrophic anthropogenic global warming want us to stop using gas @username EMOJI_police_car_light_e SUBSCRIBE TO OUR SUBSTACK : URL EMOJI_fire_e GET YOUR RAV GEAR : URL

a binary scale, such that instead of corresponding to the relative frequency of the feature, the data simply coded whether the feature was present or absent.

Subsequently, the 1,000 most frequently occurring lemmas were selected by tallying the number of texts in which each lemma appeared. Because of the use of a binary scale for the text counts, a tetrachoric correlation (Pearson, 1900) matrix was computed as input to the factor analysis. Tetrachoric correlation is a statistical method used to estimate the correlation between two dichotomously classified variables. Tetrachoric correlations were computed for the data using PROC CORR in SAS.

The next step involved processing the correlation matrix through factor analysis in SAS, leading to an initial factorial extraction. This process produced a scree plot representing the eigenvalues (see Figure 1). The guiding principle in determining the optimal number of factors is parsimony, which advocates for extracting the fewest possible factors that account for the maximum variation in data. The scree plot assists in identifying the ideal number of latent factors by indicating "elbows" in the plot line. An elbow signifies a point beyond which the addition of another factor results in a minimal increase in the explained variance (see Egbert & Staples, 2019; Friginal & Hardy, 2014).

Based on the plot shown in Figure 1, five factors were identified as a suitable number for extraction. These five factors were subsequently extracted using Promax rotation. For calculating a factor score for each post on each of the five factors, a straightforward approach was employed: The sum of variables (lemmas) loading on each factor, both positive and negative, was calculated. The

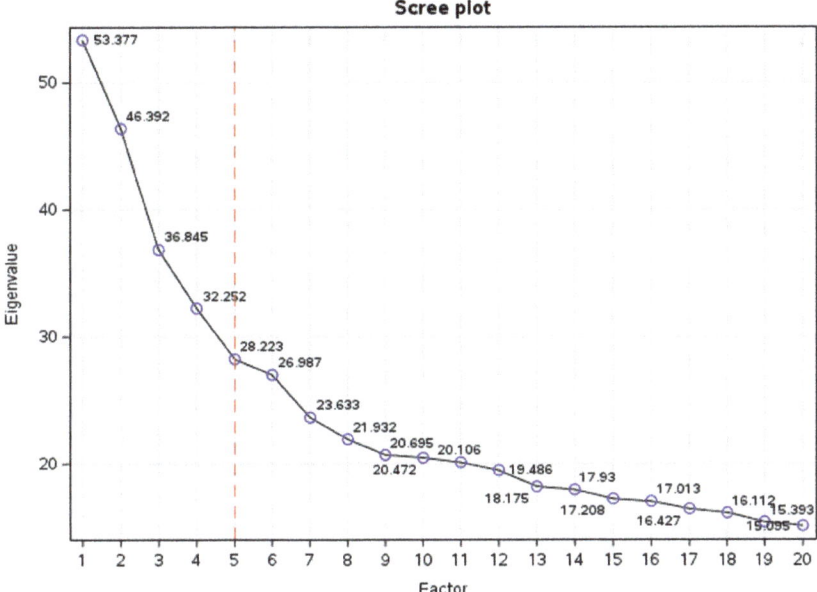

Figure 1 Scree plot of the eigenvalues of each factor.

score for a factor was determined by subtracting the total for the negative pole from that of the positive pole. In cases where lemmas loaded on multiple factors, they were included in the score computation only for the factor where they had the highest loading. For the other factors on which these lemmas loaded, the lemmas were used solely for the purpose of interpreting the factor, not for its scoring.

The qualitative interpretation of the factors involved examining multiple posts for each factor. As the data come from social media, the interpretation involved making sense of emojis, whose meanings can be fluid and often lead to misunderstandings. To aid in interpreting these emojis, we drew on Danesi (2017), who outlines that emojis perform primarily two functions in digital communication: phatic and emotive functions. For the phatic function, emojis serve to enhance the tone of digital interactions, fostering a more friendly and approachable atmosphere. The phatic function includes setting a positive opening tone, concluding messages to soften abrupt endings, and filling gaps in content, thus preventing discomfort in communication.

Conversely, the emotive function of emojis reflects emotional states in digital discourse (Danesi, 2017). For instance, emojis related to alcohol consumption can indicate a range of attitudes, from apprehension to enthusiasm. Emojis also help manage the emotional tone of the conversation, facilitating the delivery of potentially negative content in a more palatable manner.

4.3 Lexical Dimensions

In this section, the five factors are interpreted as dimensions and illustrated, as shown in Table 5.

4.3.1 Dimension 1: Discrediting Climate Change vs. Political Motivation

Table 6 lists the features identified in Factor 1. The features consist of words, emojis, and other symbols. The numbers in brackets after each feature show the factor loadings or weights. The predominant discourses on the positive pole make dense use of patriotic and ideological icons (such as the Statue of Liberty, the eagle, national flags, the cross, and the

Table 5 Dimension labels for the discourses around climate change.

Dim.	Short Labels	Long Labels
1	Discrediting Climate Change vs. Political Motivation	Discrediting Climate Change vs. International Political Motives for Climate Change Agenda
2	Activism Alarmism vs. Progressive Measures Dismissal	Framing Climate Activism as Unjustified Alarmism vs. Dismissal of Progressive Measures
3	Climate Collusion vs. Anti-Globalism	Climate Collusion Critique vs. Anti-Globalism, Criticism of Mainland China, Hypocrisy, Contradictions, and Inconsistencies in Climate Activism
4	Anti-Chinese Campaigns	Digital Media-Powered Anti-Chinese Denouncement Campaigns
5	Regulatory Agency Distrust vs. Hashtag Rejection of AGW	Business Sector Distrust of Regulatory Agencies Influenced by Climate Activism vs. Hashtag-driven Rejection of Human Influence and Corporate Responsibility

Table 6 Factor 1 Pattern.

Pole	Loadings
Positive	🅜 (1.35), 🅐 (1.35), 🌀 (1.34), 🦶 (1.34), © (1.31), ✘ (1.30), 💗 (1.30), #cog (1.28), #umpg (1.27), restriction (1.27), #dtoo (1.27), #maga (1.26), ✝ (1.24), defeat (1.20), 🧱 (1.19), gettr (1.19), ◌ (1.12), patriot (1.12), 🇧🇷 (1.11), 🌊 (1.05), 🇨🇦 (1.05), 🧡 (1.04), farming (1.01), nato (1.01), 🇮🇹 (0.99), 🌽 (0.86), 💜 (0.84), evil (0.84), (allow (0.52)), train (0.50), link (0.47), amazing (0.47), (family (0.39)), farmer (0.36)
Negative	(governance (−0.55)), china (−0.52), (environmental (−0.51)), rate (−0.42), high (−0.42), environment (−0.38), (#freemilesguo (−0.35)), (challenge (−0.35)), (cause (−0.34)), learn (−0.32), (biden (−0.32)), (issue (−0.32)), (wake (−0.32)), (ridiculous (−0.31))

letters in MAGA), carrying a nationalist, combative, and/or spiritual tone against climate change. Despite reflecting American-centered references, these messages aim to reach out to an international audience, as their overarching goal is to undermine the credibility of climate change around the world.

A notable feature of the messages marked by these discourses is a prevailing informal tone, accentuated by the dense use of emojis. Approximately 47 percent (N=17) of the variables on the positive pole are emojis. Emojis are particularly effective in communicating with diverse linguistic audiences as they overcome language barriers by not requiring linguistic proficiency for comprehension. They also add informality to messages, appealing to a wide range of digital audiences. Furthermore, emojis enhance the expressive power of the post.

Another stylistic feature of the messages influenced by this pole is the use of hashtags. Hashtags function as broadcasting devices, as they enable messages to reach large numbers of users based on specific topics. In the political arena, hashtags can act as digital "slogans" or "rally cries," fostering a sense of community and solidarity and building a solid online identity for a particular ideology.

The post in Example 1 illustrates the use of a mix of emojis and hashtags particularly targeting users from the USA, UK, Brazil, Canada, France, and Italy. It focuses on rallying a group identified as *GLOBAL PATRIOTS* and advocates for resistance against various international organizations like the

WEF, WHO, and NATO, promoting ideas of self-sufficiency in farming and water supply. The use of religious symbols and phrases such as *GOD SAVE AMERICA* intertwines patriotic and religious sentiments. Hashtags like *#patriotdrive*, *#maga*, *#winningwednesday*, and *#wwg1wga_ww* hint at an alignment with American conservative movements. The post also promotes key users, as an effort to strengthen the anti-climate change networked community around these shared beliefs and political views.

> **Example 1: Dimension 1, Positive Pole**
> 🔗 🇺🇸🇬🇧🇮🇹🇨🇦🇦🇺🇳🇿🇺🇸🔗✨GLOBAL **PATRIOTS** UNITE WITH YOUR MILITARY!! 💥🔫 RESIST THE RESET!! GET OUT OF ESG 🔥 WEF 🔥 WHO 🔥 **NATO** 🔥 GROW YOUR OWN **FARMING** AND CREATE YOUR OWN DRINKING WATER!! 🔥🔥🔥 **#cog** #warriorwednesday #dt47 **#dtoo** #fsfa **#umpg** #djt47 🇺🇸🔫🔗 GOD SAVE **AMERICA** 🇺🇸("❤️") * 🔫🔫 ❤️🇺🇸#patriotdrive **#maga** #winningwednesday #wwg1wga_ww ©🇺🇸🌷 GOD BLESS And PROTECT EVERYBODY Except Those Who Seek To Destroy **AMERICA** 🇺🇸🔫 Conductors 🎤© #jrides1 #janettrains 🔥🔥 **DEFEAT** THE **EVIL** RESET!! 🐸🔥🔥 **Gettr restrictions** 5 Riders only 🔥 FOLLOW ALL 🇺🇸🔫 @Jimmy1954 🇺🇸🇺🇸Ⓜ️🅰️🅖🅐 @titio2022 🇺🇸Ⓜ️🅰️🅖🅐 @fatima_italia 🇮🇹🇺🇸Ⓜ️🅰️🅖🅐 @Plallier 🇨🇦🇺🇸Ⓜ️🅰️🅖🅐 @Retirewcashflow 🇨🇦🇺🇸Ⓜ️🅰️🅖🅐🐎🐎🐎🐎 #jrides #jlskinstituteoflearning © Here's the **link** for your 📱 – URL

The overarching discourse of *discrediting climate change* is signaled in the texts marked by this dimension through a combination of rhetorical strategies, ideologically charged language, and specific symbols. The texts frequently use terms such as *hoax*, *evil*, *traitors*, and *globalists* to describe climate change and those who advocate for it. This language is designed to delegitimize the concept of climate change by portraying it as part of a deceptive or malevolent agenda rather than a legitimate scientific concern. The consistent use of emojis and hashtags, such as #MAGA, #Patriot, the American flag and the eagle, ties the discourse to a specific ideological community that often views climate change as a threat to personal freedom, economic stability, or national sovereignty. These symbols both signal group identity and reinforce a collective skepticism toward climate change.

Moreover, many of the texts express distrust or outright hostility toward global institutions like the World Economic Forum (WEF), environmental, social, and governance (ESG) metrics, and government policies related to climate change. Phrases such as *RESIST THE RESET*, *GET OUT OF ESG*, and *DEFEAT EVIL RESET* reflect a belief that these institutions are using climate change as a pretext for imposing restrictive or harmful policies. Additionally, some texts engage in mockery or sarcastic dismissal of climate science. For instance, one text references the impact of a blizzard on New York, sarcastically attributing it to *global warming*. This rhetorical strategy undermines the seriousness of climate change by portraying it as absurd or contradictory.

Finally, the discourse is often intertwined with the belief that climate change is being used as a tool to control or harm the population. For example, one text claims that global warming is a *scam* used by *globalists* to wipe out independent farmers, thus linking climate change rhetoric to a broader agenda of global control.

In contrast, the negative pole corresponds to a sharply distinct style compared to the positive pole. The posts on the negative pole typically adopt a more formal tone, often lacking emojis and hashtags (see Example 2). While emojis constitute 47.2 percent of the variables on the positive pole, and hashtags 11 percent, in the negative pole, these elements represent only 7.1 percent of the variables, with just one hashtag. The primary focus of these messages is to express opposition to "globalist ideologies" in general, and more specifically, to accuse China of hypocritical behavior, criticizing its environmental pollution practices while simultaneously supporting climate change initiatives abroad as a means to achieve global dominance. Often, these criticisms are directed toward the Chinese Communist Party (CCP) and its alleged manipulation of climate change narratives.

> **Example 2: Dimension 1, Negative Pole**
> Nicole on Wayne Dupree Show: **China** is the world's biggest polluter with **high** cancer incidence and suicidal **rate** so it is **ridiculous** to work with the CCP on climate change. In fact, the agenda on the global **challenge** of climate change is not about protecting the **environment** but a smokescreen for the CCP and the globalists' ambition to establish a new world order and global **governance**. **#freemilesguo** #freeyvettewang

The text exemplifies the discourse of political motivation by framing China's role in global climate change discussions as a facade for more sinister political ambitions. It portrays the CCP and *globalists* as using climate change as a *smokescreen* to pursue a *new world order*, rather than genuinely addressing environmental concerns. The emphasis on governance, both in the specific mention of global governance and in the broader context of the intentions behind the CCP, is aimed at viewing climate change policies as tools for political control rather than genuine efforts to protect the environment.

4.3.2 Dimension 2: Activism Alarmism vs. Progressive Measures Dismissal

As indicated by the terms in Table 7, the underlying discourses on the positive pole focus on a general skepticism against scientific climate change predictions that are branded as "alarmist."

Table 7 Factor 2 Pattern.

Pole	Loadings
Positive	temperature (0.96), earth (0.88), scientist (0.85), warm (0.84), weather (0.82), warming (0.82), dioxide (0.81), atmosphere (0.80), decade (0.80), hot (0.79), ice (0.79), age (0.79), science (0.77), heat (0.76), lie (0.75), anthropogenic (0.75), man (0.74), natural (0.73), hoax (0.71), data (0.71), carbon (0.67), alarmist (0.66), fake (0.64), degree (0.64), planet (0.64), cooling (0.63), narrative (0.63), emergency (0.63), rise (0.62), human (0.62), evidence (0.62), made (0.61), emission (0.58), wind (0.57), cause (0.56), global (0.55), #climatechange (0.51), fire (0.49), geologist (0.49), year (0.49), mongering (0.47), continued (0.46), gore (0.44), 😂 (0.44), (amazing (0.44)), car (0.44), surface (0.44), #globalwarming (0.43), population (0.42), idiot (0.41), media (0.40), (united (0.39)), blame (0.39), climate (0.37), threat (0.37), shit (0.37), gates (0.36), bullshit (0.35), 😡 (0.35), existential (0.34), #climatehoax (0.34), #climatechangehoax (0.33), agw (0.33), crime (0.33), (#climate (0.33)), average (0.32), 😉 (0.31), toxic (0.31), era (0.31), covid (0.30), 💩 (0.30), author (0.30).
Negative	governance (−0.78), esg (−0.78), larry (−0.70), fink (−0.67), (blackrock (−0.62)), index (−0.60), (retirement (−0.56)), (social (−0.56)), cei (−0.56), (executive (−0.55)), corporate (−0.55), #esg (−0.53), vanguard (−0.53), metric (−0.53), (fiduciary (−0.51)), weaponized (−0.51), pension (−0.50), equity (−0.49), progressive (−0.48), epochtv (−0.48), shadow (−0.46), #dei (−0.44), #blackrock (−0.44), treasurer (−0.43), diversity (−0.43), stocklin (−0.43), participate (−0.42), inclusion (−0.41), esghurt (−0.41), (board (−0.41)), attorney (−0.41), (asset (−0.40)), committee (−0.40), firm (−0.39), (manager (−0.38)), (invest (−0.38)), (credit (−0.38)), shareholder (−0.38), rating (−0.37), (financial (−0.36)), feature (−0.35), (desantis (−0.35)), (nicole (−0.35)), (labor (−0.33)), finance (−0.33), antichrist (−0.33), target (−0.32), (stake (−0.32)), institution (−0.32), racket (−0.32), banking (−0.32), (wayne (−0.30))

The posts introduce and dispute these claims through a range of communicative mechanisms, such as belittling opposing media narratives, questioning scientific consensus, cherry-picking historical precedents, and promoting data-driven doubt (see Example 3). These discourses are marked by scientific terms such as *temperature, earth, scientist, atmosphere,* and *carbon,* reflecting core elements of climate science. Lemmas like *warming, dioxide, ice,* and *emissions* specifically address aspects of the ongoing debate about the causes and effects of climate change. As mentioned, a notable aspect of the discourses is put in place through emotionally charged terms, such as *hoax, lie, fake,* and *alarmist,* whose goal is the outright rejection of the consensus in climate science. In addition, lemmas like *narrative, media, and alarmist* suggest a focus on the alleged misleading portrayal of climate change in public discourse and the media. Like the positive pole on the previous factor, the variables also include casual or emotive expressions (e.g., 😂, *shit,* 😡), indicating a strong emotional component in these discussions. Names like *Gore* and mentions of other global issues like *covid* suggest connections made between climate change and broader political or social contexts, often portrayed as being interconnected by some form of worldwide conspiracy against the West.

> **Example 3: Dimension 2, Positive Pole**
> **Scientists** seeking funding and journalists seeking an audience agree: PANIC SELLS. Here's the **continued** list – an **amazing** chronology of the last 120 **years** of scare-mongering on **climate** • 1938 – **Global warming**, **caused** by **man heating** the **planet** with **carbon dioxide**, 'is likely to prove beneficial to **mankind** in several ways, besides the provision of **heat** and power.' – Quarterly Journal of the Royal Meteorological Society • 1938 . . .

On the negative pole, by contrast, the prevailing discourses center around skepticism toward climate advocacy-led corporate measures, which takes shape through a narrative contrasting the weakening of the West with the strengthening of China, fears of the loss of the global dominance of Western powers, allegations of corporate tyranny, and even the presence of anti-Semitic connotations (see Example 4). Corporate governance and investment practices are indexed through terms like *governance, ESG, corporate,* and *pension.* Mention of influential figures and entities in the financial world are constant, through terms such as *Larry Fink, BlackRock,* and *Vanguard.* The discourses also rely on financial terminology, such *index, metric, shareholder,* and *investment.* The posts often refer critically to social justice agendas through terms like *diversity, inclusion, equity,* and *progressive.* Political and legal aspects are also referenced, with terms like *attorney, treasurer,* and *committee.*

> **Example 4: Dimension 2, Negative Pole**
> **Larry Fink** – **BlackRock** CEO – #wef **Board** of Trustees "Well, behaviors are going to have to change. And this is one thing we are asking companies . . . you have force behaviors. At **BlackRock** we are forcing behaviors." **#fink**

weaponizes $10,000,000,000,000 (ten trillion) of your **pension** funds to push **ESG** (Environmental, **Social & Governance**) scores and **CEI** (Corp Equality **Index**) scores as a **corporate social credit** system. The result is a weakened West relative to a strengthened China. This is #greatrest for #agenda2030.

The dimensions present partial similarities, which indicates the employment of different communicative strategies to convey the same basic ideology of climate change denial. Therefore, the overlaps do not indicate exact repetition, but different shapes of the same ideological discourse.

One such similarity exists between the positive poles of Dimension 1 and Dimension 2, where combative and emotionally charged lexis and iconographic forms are used. However, the distinction lies in their application: Dimension 1 employs these terms in a broader, ideological context, while Dimension 2 focuses specifically on the scientific aspects, questioning the validity of climate science and the portrayal of climate change in the media.

4.3.3 Dimension 3: Climate Collusion vs. Anti-Globalism

The predominant discourses on the positive pole (see Table 8) refer to what is perceived as the meddling of climate activism ideology in business affairs (see Example 5). This takes various forms in the posts, including assertions of collusion between political and industrial entities, accusations of capital losses caused by ESG policies, the politicization of banking systems, the perception of disregard for US interests, and the suggestion of a destructive agenda by the US presidency. The economic focus is evident through such lemmas as *company*, *invest*, and *investment*. Terms like *social*, *ESG*, and *BlackRock* suggest a specific concern with the introduction of social responsibility and environmental, social, and governance (ESG) demands in the context of business practices. Terms like *market*, *asset*, *fiduciary*, and *financial* further accentuate the market economy lens through which climate change is viewed. Additionally, terms like *risk*, *strategy*, and *security* point to a focus on the management side of business. The political facet of the discourse is indexed through terms such as *Republican* and *Biden*.

> **Example 5: Dimension 3, Positive Pole**
> **ESG** index funds have underperformed the broader **market** over the last few years while costing 5x more to own and a volatile **risk** to add to one's long term **investment** goals Vetoing the bill is contrary to what **Biden** is **stating** by not giving **fiduciaries** the option to choose whether or not to opt in to adding so-called **ESG companies** into one's **retirement account**.

Table 8 Factor 3 Pattern.

Pole	Loadings
Positive	company (0.92), invest (0.91), (investment (0.89)), social (0.81), american (0.77), allow (0.76), (esg (0.76)), wake (0.75), policy (0.73), blackrock (0.72), asset (0.70), state (0.70), (market (0.69)), decision (0.68), environmental (0.68), issue (0.68), republican (0.67), (investor (0.66)), retirement (0.65), manager (0.63), bank (0.63), corporation (0.62), business (0.62), financial (0.61), lead (0.60), influence (0.60), fiduciary (0.59), consider (0.58), factor (0.58), national (0.55), part (0.55), bit (0.53), biden (0.51), general (0.51), labor (0.50), fossil (0.50), practice (0.50), (evil (0.49)), credit (0.49), agenda (0.48), (america (0.48)), (#esg (0.48)), demand (0.47), economic (0.46), (corporate (0.46)), explain (0.45), society (0.44), (security (0.44)), united (0.43), desantis (0.43), (human (0.43)), risk (0.42), (link (0.42)), (watch (0.40)), (strategy (0.40)), states (0.38), account (0.37), (fink (0.36)), (👎 (0.36)), (firm (0.36)), (group (0.35)), (treasurer (0.34)), (man (0.33)), (car (0.33)), radical (0.32), electric (0.32), (earth (0.32)), (announce (0.31)), (population (0.30))
Negative	wayne (−0.67), suicidal (−0.62), climatique (−0.62), nicole (−0.60), incidence (−0.59), 😱 (−0.59), palestine (−0.55), wreak (−0.55), havoc (−0.55), thunberg (−0.52), ridiculous (−0.49), la (−0.49), ohio (−0.49), greta (−0.48), icebound (−0.47), 🤢 (−0.46), cancer (−0.46), harry (−0.46), 🤮 (−0.45), challenge (−0.44), east (−0.44), ambition (−0.43), 😨 (−0.41), confine (−0.41), snowflake (−0.41), establish (−0.40), 🙊 (−0.40), (#freeyvettewang (−0.39)), 🐀 (−0.37), search (−0.36), anchor (−0.36), arrive (−0.36), ♂ (−0.36), change (−0.36), corollavirus (−0.35), livesmatter (−0.35), greenpeace (−0.35), polar (−0.35), (climate (−0.34)), tropics (−0.34), messiah (−0.34), deepstate (−0.34), demoncrap (−0.33), (🇫🇷 (−0.33)), #klausschwab (−0.32), ™ (−0.31), coverage (−0.31), prince (−0.31), (🙄(−0.30)), shape (−0.30)

The negative pole conveys discourses aligned with anti-globalism in general, anti-Chinese influence, and hypocrisy of climate advocates in particular. These general discourse coordinates filter down to various political messages, such as endorsing Chinese dissidents, voicing anger against global governance, alleging mainstream media bias, and bolstering the viewpoints of anti-CCP podcast and talk show hosts (see Example 6). The variables include proper nouns such as *Wayne*, *Nicole*, *Greta*, and *Thunberg* referring to media personalities involved in the climate change debate. *Climatique* is part of the phrase *changement climatique*, French for *climate change*, found in bilingual posts. Lemmas like *suicidal*, *ridiculous*, *wreak*, and *havoc*, and emojis such as 😨 and 🤢 illustrate an emotive or dramatic tone often employed in these messages.

> **Example 6: Dimension 3, Negative Pole**
> **Nicole** on **Wayne** Dupree Show: China is the world's biggest polluter with high **cancer incidence** and **suicidal** rate so it is **ridiculous** to work with the CCP on **climate change**. In fact, the agenda on the global **challenge** of **climate change** is not about protecting the environment but a smokescreen for the CCP and the globalists' **ambition** to **establish** a new world order and global governance.

A partial overlap exists between the negative poles of Dimensions 3 and 1. Both express doubts about the efficacy and intentions of global climate initiatives. The variation here is in their focal points – Dimension 1 gravitates toward a general opposition to globalist ideologies, while Dimension 3 centers more specifically on the role and influence of China in these global frameworks, highlighting a narrower, more targeted form of skepticism.

4.3.4 Dimension 4: Anti-Chinese Campaigns

Unlike previous factors, Factor 4 has a single pole (see Table 9), with an underlying discourse based on voicing concerns about the global impact of the CCP's actions. These concerns are supported primarily by quoting digital media sources that are critical of the CCP and their manipulation of foreign

Table 9 Factor 4 Pattern.

Pole	Loadings
Positive	#freemilesguo (1.35), matta (1.34), blackstone (1.34), kleptocrats (1.34), mining (1.32), #freeyvettewang (1.32), citic (1.29), ivanhoe (1.26), acquire (1.24), stake (1.21), january (1.16), strategy (1.15), family (1.12), announce (1.10), canadian (1.06), #ccp (1.00), investment (0.89), group (0.89), (company (0.72)), time (0.62)
Negative	No variables

economies. The posts largely denounce the alleged wrongdoings of the CCP and the growing worldwide influence of China. Because the intended audience includes Chinese speakers, the typical posts are bilingual, written in both English and Chinese (see Example 7).

The hashtag #freemilesguo is associated with Miles Guo, a Chinese billionaire and whistleblower, who is involved in anti-CCP activities and has connections with former Trump advisor Steve Bannon. The hashtag refers to a campaign for his release or support, particularly from those who view his treatment by legal authorities as unjust. In turn, the term *Matta* relates to a web TV show hosted by Ryan Matta, who has a significant digital presence in the conservative movement. Matta is known for supporting Donald Trump and is actively involved in the "America First Movement." Variables such as *blackstone* and *kleptocrats* suggest a focus on personal or corporate responsibility. Terms like *mining*, *citic*, and *Ivanhoe* point toward an interest in particular economic sectors. Additionally, lemmas like *acquire*, *stake*, *company*, *investment*, and *strategy* indicate an economic focus, emphasizing business maneuvers and financial aspects. The presence of Canadian and *#ccp* implies an international reach.

> **Example 7: Dimension 4, Positive Pole**
> 06. 29 [Ava on The Ryan **Matta** Show-04] CITIC **Group**, which is owned by several CCP **kleptocrats families**, **acquired** a 20% **stake** in **Canadian company**, **Ivanhoe Mining**, in 2018, and **Blackstone announced** its ESG **investment strategy** for the first **time** in **January** 2020. #chinese≠ccp #nfsc #takedowntheccp #**freemilesguo** #**freeyvettewang** 多个中共盗国贼家族拥有的中信集团2018年收购加拿大Ivanhoe矿业20\%的股份,2020年1月黑石首次宣布ESG投资策略.

An overlap can be seen here between Dimension 4 and the negative pole of Dimension 1, as both engage in criticism of Chinese environmental policies and global influence. Yet, the emphasis differs: Dimension 1 is more directly aligned with geopolitical criticism, whereas Dimension 4 extends this criticism to a broader denouncement of the CCP, incorporating a global perspective and a broader critique of international politics.

4.3.5 Dimension 5: Regulatory Agency Distrust vs. Hashtag Rejection of AGW

The positive pole incorporates discourses questioning the validity of advocacy in general and highlighting the disconnect between climate change advocacy and business expertise in particular, exposing contradictions in the stance of anti-fossil fuel members on oil company boards, and criticizing what is seen as

Table 10 Factor 5 Pattern.

Pole	Loadings
Positive	exchange (1.27), commission (1.27), disclosure (1.23), requirement (1.23), abuse (1.18), provide (1.17), chairman (1.16), director (1.14), failure (1.14), illegal (1.13), proposal (1.13), list (1.11), security (1.08), agency (1.07), replace (1.04), suggest (1.03), board (0.96), executive (0.94), investor (0.80), market (0.72), (time (0.46))
Negative	#wef (−0.47), 👎 (−0.44), #agenda2030 (−0.41), #climatecrisis (−0.38), #climate (−0.38), (#climatechange (−0.36)), (cancer (−0.35)), (larry (−0.35)), #greatreset (−0.35), (establish (−0.34)), (#globalwarming (−0.34)), (#climatehoax (−0.33)), #woke (−0.33), (explain (−0.32)), (incidence (−0.31)), (#blackrock (−0.30)), #globalwarminghoax (−0.30), (suicidal (−0.30)), (anthropogenic (−0.30))

exaggerated climate change rhetoric (see Table 10). In general, this translates into a discourse of distrust from business sectors toward economic agencies that support climate change activism (see Example 8). For instance, *exchange* and *commission* refer to the Securities and Exchange Commission (SEC), a US government agency responsible for regulating the securities markets and protecting investors. Terms like *disclosure* and *requirement* suggest a demand for transparency and accountability in climate-related actions and policies. The employment of *abuse*, *illegal*, and *failure* questions the legitimacy and effectiveness of climate advocacy, disputing the connection between climate change credentials and business leadership. Additionally, terms such as *chairman*, *director*, and *executive* highlight a scrutiny of the roles and actions of individuals in leadership positions, particularly in relation to anti-fossil fuel entities. The presence of lemmas like *proposal*, *list*, and *security* further reflects a detailed examination of the strategies and policies proposed by climate advocates, while terms like *agency*, *board*, and *investor* emphasize the diverse range of stakeholders involved.

> **Example 8: Dimension 5, Positive Pole**
> The spokesperson pointed out the **failures** and **abuses** of power by the **Chairman** of the **Securities** and **Exchange Commission**, Gensler, and **suggested** the need to restructure the **agency**. The article **listed** some of the **abuses**, including proposing too many rule **proposals**, **providing** inappropriate comment periods, and unworkable and **illegal** ESG **disclosure requirements**. . . .

In contrast, the negative pole shifts away from the alleged negative interference of climate activism in business to a broader denial of the existence of climate change (see Example 9). These discourses often manifest through the use of platform-specific tags and cultural and ideological labels, underscoring skepticism toward proposed solutions and reinforcing a general discourse of rejecting human influence and corporate responsibility. For instance, the use of hashtags such as *#climatehoax* and *#globalwarminghoax* directly questions the validity of climate science. In turn, *#wef* and *#agenda2030* suggest resistance to widely accepted environmental agendas and initiatives. Additionally, *#greatreset* and *#woke* indicate a broader cultural and ideological opposition that extends beyond environmental issues. The term *Great Reset* originally emerged from the 2020 World Economic Forum (WEF) meeting in response to the COVID-19 pandemic. The WEF proposed it as a way to rebuild the global economy in a more sustainable and equitable manner post-pandemic, involving curbing climate change, reimagining social contracts, and shifting toward more inclusive economic models. However, critics have used the term to mean a plan by global elites to control the world.

Example 9: Dimension 5, Negative Pole
MAN DOES NOT EFFECT C02 IN THE ATMOSPHERE Indisputable proof below from Australian Senator Malcolm Roberts ✵ REPOST ✵ REPOST ✵ REPOST DOWNLOAD AND SHARE TO THE CLIMATE CHANGE NUTS **#climatehoax** #climatelies **#climatechange #climatecrisis #climate** #climatechangehoax **#globalwarminghoax #globalwarming** #globalwarminglie @Nigel_Farage @TommyRobinson1 @gettrUK @TogetherDec @TuckerCarlson #gettrnews #gettr #gettrnews #gettrnewsonline #gettrusa #gettrbrasil #gettrretro #gettrgaming #gettrdeutschland #depopulation #depopulationagenda **#wef** **#wef** #wefagenda2030 **#agenda2030**.

As with the other dimensions, a partial overlap is found here between the negative pole of Dimension 5 and the positive pole of Dimension 1, both of which share the same overarching goal of discrediting climate change as a whole. The difference is that while both exhibit a denial of climate change, Dimension 1 is more general, representing anger and popular sentiment, whereas Dimension 5 is more specific, repelling climate activism based on business credentials.

In addition, both of these poles adopt an informal, sketchy style, achieved through different means: whereas in Dimension 1 this is achieved by a dense use of emojis, in Dimension 5 this is accomplished through repeated use of hashtags.

4.4 Synthesis and Discussion

Albeit numerous, the dimensions converge on a limited set of formations: business, Sinophobia (the fear and distrust of China), and science denial, each representing a distinct focus of anti-climate advocacy ideology.

First, three dimensions are connected by a focus on business, each presenting a specific emphasis, ranging from geopolitical implications and corporate governance to the interplay between climate activism and business operations. Dimension 2 (negative pole) focuses on skepticism toward climate advocacy-led corporate measures, with narratives emphasizing the decline of Western global dominance and the rise of China. In contrast, the positive pole of Dimension 3 deals with the interference of climate activism in business affairs. Here, the discourse centers on the alleged collusion between political and industrial entities and the negative impact of ESG policies on capital. This pole frequently employs economic terminology, reflecting concerns about the introduction of social responsibility demands in business practices and the politicization of economic systems. Dimension 5 (positive pole), on the other hand, questions the legitimacy of climate change advocacy and its alignment with business expertise. The discourse here is marked by a demand for transparency and accountability in climate-related policies and actions, with a focus on the scrutiny of strategies and policies proposed by climate advocates.

Second, Sinophobia is mobilized using three different dimensions, collectively portraying China as a hypocritical and dominating force in global climate politics. In Dimension 1 (negative pole), the focus is on opposing globalist ideologies, particularly criticizing China for its environmental policies while paradoxically supporting climate change initiatives abroad, suggesting a strategy for global dominance. In Dimension 3 (negative pole), the discourse is aligned with anti-globalism and anti-Chinese influence, manifesting in various political messages that include endorsing Chinese dissidents and voicing anger against global governance. And in Dimension 4 (positive pole), the discourse voices concerns about the global impact of CCP actions, often citing digital media sources critical of manipulation of foreign economies by the CCP.

Finally, science denial is evoked primarily in (the positive pole of) Dimension 2, where scientific research is represented negatively in different ways, such as being manipulated, erratic, or alarmist. The discourse here implies that the scientific community lacks the proper credentials to provide unbiased and reliable information on climate change, suggesting that their findings are driven more by personal or political agendas than by objective scientific inquiry (e.g., "Scientists seeking funding" from Example 3).

As shown, the blend of discourses that forms the basis of anti-climate advocacy is largely a process of articulation, through the use of different facets of similar discourses. Articulation is defined by Cini (2000, p. 4) as "a process which brings together elements of existing discourses in a new and more legitimate formation." This process involves the joining, linking, associating, and structuring of various discourse elements, as described by Haye and Larraín (2018, p. 78), who perceive articulation as "the creation of a contingent new reality from what already exists." In short, as Fairclough (2003, p. 127) sees it, "[t]he new is made out of a novel articulation of the old."

Affiliation to a movement, such as anti-climate action, is not primarily rooted in logical demonstration but rather in fostering a sense of community around a cause. The effectiveness of such a movement depends more on its capacity to politicize public opinion than on the inherent plausibility of its ideas: "The power of a discourse depends less on its intrinsic properties than on the mobilizing power it exercises—that is, at least to some extent on the degree to which it is recognized by a numerous and powerful group that can recognize itself in it" (Bourdieu, 1991, p. 188).

Furthermore, this case study shows that dimensions found in LMDA can have counterparts in dimensions identified in TMDA. As described, Dimension 1 distinguishes between formal and informal styles in digital messaging, identifying informal styles through significant use of emojis and hashtags, in contrast to formal styles that use regular prose and specialized vocabulary.

This division between formal and informal broadly corresponds to similar distinctions found in previous TMDA studies. For instance, Biber (1988) uncovered a distinction between involved and informational communication, where the former, akin to the positive pole of the current Dimension 1, is typically less formal and more conversational, while the latter, similar to the negative pole, is more detached and written-like.

Berber Sardinha's studies (2022b, 2022c) also identified related dimensions in social media communication. In Berber Sardinha (2022b), two dimensions were described: "formal, informational, argumentative discourse," aligning with the negative pole of the current Dimension 1, and "informal, interactive, speaker-oriented discourse," which mirrors the positive pole. Berber Sardinha (2022c) determined three similar dimensions: "formal, prepared, informational communication" corresponding to the negative pole, with "informal, interactive, stance-marked discourse" and "expression of personal attitudes and feelings" reflecting the broader range of informal communication captured by the positive pole of the current Dimension 1.

4.5 Conclusion

Our analysis offers a comprehensive examination of the diverse ideological narratives pervading right-wing anti-climate advocacy on GETTR. This analysis identified nine distinct discourses, each marked by specific dimension poles that illustrate the variety of strategies employed by the movement. These strategies encompass allegations of business malpractice and corruption, both at local and international levels, assertions of geopolitical manipulation, accusations of scientific misconduct, and expressions of nationalistic pride.

Further, the case study highlights how these discourses manifest through varied messaging styles – from the use of emotive emojis and strategic hashtags to narrative techniques seen in expository writing, news formats, and popular science presentations. Despite the diversity in presentation, a common ideological thread emerges, centered around three pivotal themes: business interests, Sinophobia, and science denial. These themes not only scaffold the overarching frame within this community but also shape the ideological constructs that define this movement.

5 Case Study 2: Exploring the Distribution of Selected Migrant Education Ideological Discourses Over Time and Register

Shannon Fitzsimmons-Doolan

5.1 Introduction

As presented in Section 1, discourses are higher-order, latent constructs indexed by and across language that influence and are influenced by shared social meanings. Discourses range from more neutral phenomena, indicative of topics or themes, to more ideological phenomena which convey socially shared beliefs (Fitzsimmons-Doolan, 2023). Like all linguistic systems, discourses are understood to have structured variation in distribution. Because they are socially co-constructed, such variation may be tied to situational characteristics of text production. The case study presented in this section extends an LMDA study (Fitzsimmons-Doolan, 2023) to explore the distribution of ideological discourses by register and time.

Fitzsimmons-Doolan (2023), one of the LMDA studies presented in Section 2, applied LMDA to the US Migrant Education Corpus, a multi-register corpus of twenty-first-century texts on the topic of migrant education. One of the primary inclusion criteria for the lexical variables in the study was a grammatical role of evaluation or modification of the node *MIGR*. This criterion allowed the identified factors to be operationalized as ideological discourses about (im)migrants/(im)migration. Using the quantitative values generated from that analysis, this case study extends that inquiry to better understand how text register and publication date, taken both separately and together, may have influenced the distribution of four of the eleven ideological discourses identified in the original study.

Scholarship suggests a strong relationship between register (Biber and Conrad, 2019) and the distribution of (ideological) discourses. In his theory of lexical priming, Hoey (2005) argues that lexical collocation (the fundamental relationship on which LMDA and its outputs are based) involves the "cumulative" loading of "contents and co-texts in which it [a word] is encountered" (p. 8). Based on a survey of past studies, Biber (2012) demonstrates that register is an important source of variation for lexical, grammatical, and lexico-grammatical levels of language. Since we argue that (ideological) discourses can be derived through LMDA, it would hold that register would be a source of variation in the distribution of discourses. Moreover, Jaworska and Kinloch (2018) note that (1) discourse production is constrained by context, (2) discourse travels across contexts, and (3) empirical investigation is needed to observe how "a discursive phenomenon 'behaves' across contexts" (p. 111). Following up on these claims, Crossley and Louwerse (2007) found that dimensions based on clusters of bigrams could classify registers, while Berber Sardinha (2017) found that registers predicted collocations. Furthermore, several studies have also found differences in representations of (im)migrants/(im)migration by register:

- Representations of RASIM varied by newspaper register (i.e., tabloids, broadsheets, national newspapers, regional papers) (Blinder & Allen, 2016; Taylor, 2014).[1]
- Representations of asylum seekers varied between national newspapers versus local news websites (Bates, 2017).
- Representations of migrants varied between legislation texts versus administrative texts (Peréz-Paredes et al., 2017).

Thus, it is hypothesized that register will account for variation in the distribution of ideological discourses in the US Migrant Education Corpus.

Less scholarship has focused on the distribution of (ideological) discourses over time, though linguistic change over time is obviously a well-established area of inquiry and corpus linguistics approaches have been used to investigate such change. Modern diachronic corpus-assisted discourse studies is a subfield which compares corpora across time to reveal, among other phenomena, "non-obvious meaning" (a construct consistent with discourses) across texts within a

---

[1] RASIM = Refugees, asylum seekers, and immigrants

register (Partington, 2010, p. 88). Many projects using the SiBol corpus of newspaper texts over multiple decades have identified changing representation of socially important topics (e.g., morality) over time (Marchi, 2018). Finally, multiple studies investigating the representation of (im)migrants/(im)migration over time, particularly through metaphor, have identified change (Santa Ana et al., 2007; Taylor, 2014, 2021).

Limited work has explored the role of time and register together in the distribution of (ideological) discourses. Gal (2018) notes that "discourse seems to 'move' or spread across speech events" (p. 67) and emphasizes the "open-ended" (p. 67), dynamic nature of discourses over time, suggesting that studies of discourses should attend to both situational context (e.g., register) and time, as well as the interplay between the two variables. Taylor (2018) used newspaper texts and parliamentary proceedings over seven decades to document change in the representation of the same cohort of immigrants over time and across registers. Through this analysis, she found little overlap in the representation of the cohort over time, but identified similarities in how "new" verses established cohorts of immigrants were represented. Stewart et al. (2011) contrasted levels of discursive tone across register (news, editorial, and letters to the editor texts) and over time in local newspaper texts about "illegal immigrants" (p. 8). They found significant differences for both register and time in language describing everyday life. Finally, Santa Ana et al. (2007) claim that positive metaphors about immigrants (e.g., IMMIGRANTS ARE HUMAN, IMMIGRANTS ARE WORKERS, IMMIGRANTS ARE CONTRIBUTORS) originated in immigrants-rights communities in the 1990s and were then deployed by then President George W. Bush beginning in 2004. The authors suggest use of such metaphors by a US president was publicly legitimizing and may account for the dramatic increase in their use in newspaper texts (from 2.3 percent of metaphors in 1999 to 42 percent of metaphors in 2006).

Given the findings that both register and time separately and together may account for variation, this case study asks, *What patterns related to register and time are apparent in the distribution of four ideological discourses about migrant education?*

5.2 Methodology

To address the research question, several inferential statistical tests were conducted using values per text for each of four ideological discourses identified in the US Migrant Education Corpus. Texts were also coded by register (comment, regional newspaper, national newspaper, state Department of Education (DOE) webtext, federal DOE webtext) and year. The following sections explain the corpus makeup, operationalization of ideological discourses, as well as the analysis design for this study.

5.2.1 US Migrant Education Corpus

The US Migrant Education Corpus is a 9.2-million-word corpus of texts from online newspaper comments, US regional and national newspapers, selected state DOE webtexts, and the federal DOE webtexts about migrant education in the US published between 2003 and 2018. Table 11 presents an overview of the corpus made up of three general registers: online newspaper comments, newspaper articles, and DOE webtexts with two general registers further subdivided into more specific registers (regional and national newspapers; state and federal DOE webtexts), resulting in five register categories in total. The online newspaper comments are two complete comment threads (2009, 2016) in response to published newspaper texts about migrant education. The regional and national

Table 11 US Migrant Education Corpus Overview.

Register Subcorpus	Sources	Years	Total Word Count
Online Newspaper Comments	New York Times, Washington Post	2009, 2016	197,530
Regional Newspapers	Chicago Tribune, Denver Post, Houston Chronicle, Los Angeles Times	2003–17	785,491
National Newspapers	New York Times, USA Today, Wall Street Journal	2003–17	496,738
States' DOE	California DOE migrant education office, California DOE office of English acquisition, Delaware DOE migrant education office, Delaware DOE office of English acquisition	2004-5, 2012–13, 2017–18	2,072,707
Federal DOE	The Office of Migrant Education, The Office of English Acquisition	2004–5, 2012–13, 2017–18	5,690,303

newspaper subcorpora include all of the articles between 2003 and 2017 that include the terms education and (immigration or immigrant) identified through library databases. The state and federal DOE subcorpora include all texts three clicks away from the migrant education or English language acquisition office homepages (2005, 2013, 2018) archived by the Wayback Machine (2001) on January 1 of that respective year.[2] (See Fitzsimmons-Doolan (2023) for more on the composition of the corpus.)

5.2.2 Ideological Discourses

As presented in Section 2 of this Element, Fitzsimmons-Doolan (2023) identified and described eleven ideological discourses from the US Migrant Education Corpus. The discourses were operationalized as the qualitative interpretation of factors resulting from an LMDA of the distribution of a set of lexical variables (e.g., services, officials, law, working) that evaluated or modified words containing the root *MIGR* in the corpus.

To select the focal discourses for this exploratory analysis, the author identified four discourses that, *together*, would best help answer this question in a meaningful way because of their variability of distribution in the corpus (i.e., total variance accounted for), variability in saliency in particular registers (based on descriptive data), and potential to influence applied scholarship. Thus, the distribution of four ideological discourses – (1) *Government programs serve children in need*, (2) *Immigrant lives are narratives (usually criminal or uplifting)*, (3) *Top-down immigration laws are punitive or permissive*, and (4) *Immigrants and governments have a mutual relationship founded on acts of service and work* – were chosen as the focus of this exploratory study. Regression factor scores from the LMDA were used as the measure of the strength of each focal ideological discourse per text.

5.2.3 Analysis Design

Because the four focal ideological discourses were extracted using an orthogonal rotation, they are considered independent of one another. This claim was confirmed by examining their pooled within-group correlations. Because of this, the analysis of the distribution of each ideological discourse by register and time had to be taken discourse by discourse in four separate analyses. Furthermore, while each of the five registers was represented for each

---

[2] Because of the archiving procedures of the Wayback Machine, many of the pages three clicks away from the node pages (archived in 2005, 2013, and 2018) were, in fact, archived in the previous year (2004, 2012, 2017, respectively). Therefore, the three time periods of data for the state and federal DOE webtexts are 2004–5, 2012–13, and 2017–18.

ideological discourse, time was not sampled in the same way for each register type. That is, only two years (2009, 2016) were sampled for online newspaper comments, fifteen years were sampled for newspaper articles (2003–17), and three time periods were sampled for DOE texts (2004–5, 2012–13, 2017–18). Thus, any analysis including both time and register as variables for a given ideological discourse had to be broken down into three separate analyses (i.e., comments, newspaper articles, DOE webtexts). However, it was possible to get an overall picture of register only for each ideological discourse.

Figure 2 presents an overview of the analysis design of the study. For each ideological discourse, first a test was conducted comparing the averages of each of the five registers to understand the distribution of the ideological discourse by register independent of time. Then, in order to understand the distribution of the ideological discourse in the corpus, taking both time and register into account in relation to one another, three additional analyses were conducted – one comparing the factor score averages of texts grouped by year for comment texts, one comparing the factor score averages of texts grouped by year and newspaper registers for newspaper texts, and one comparing the factor score averages of texts grouped by time period and DOE registers for DOE texts (Field, 2013). Unless otherwise reported, all assumptions were checked and met. For each comparison across all five registers, because the assumption of equality of

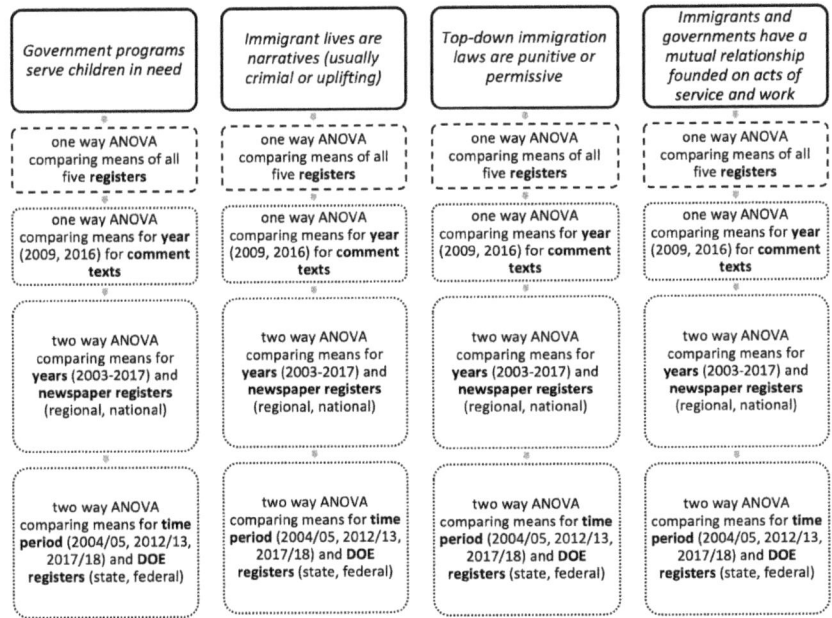

Figure 2 Overview of analysis design.

variance was not met, the Welch test statistic was used to determine significance and the Games-Howell statistic was used for the post hoc comparisons. The alpha for each of the tests was set at 0.0021 for an experiment-wise error rate for all planned analyses for this dataset of 0.05.[3]

5.3 Results

5.3.1 Government Programs Serve Children in Need

This ideological discourse is expressed in texts about government programs for whom youth, presented as needy, are the target beneficiaries. The lexical items *services, youth, provide, programs, health, children, state, education, assist, center, ensure, information, needs, child, office, including,* and *comprehensive* co-occur to express this ideological discourse, as in the following example from a regional newspaper text.

> **Example 1**
> Metropolitan Family **Services** has operated a Head Start **program** in the Chicago Lawn community on the city's Southwest Side. The 1-, 2-, 3-, and 4-year-old **children** we serve each year are all poor. Most are born to <u>immigrant</u> families with limited English literacy. Ten percent have physical or cognitive disabilities.

5.3.1.1 Variation in Register Distribution

A one-way ANOVA was conducted to examine the relationship between register and representation of the ideological discourse, *Government programs serve children in need*. The independent variable was register (comment, regional newspaper, national newspaper, state DOE webtext, and federal DOE webtext). The dependent variable was the factor score per each of the corpus texts ($n = 3,809$) for this discourse. Figure 3 shows the average factor score per register for this ideological discourse. Figure 4 shows significant differences and the effect sizes of those differences among the five registers for this ideological discourse. Figure 5 shows the factor scores for each register over time. The test revealed a statistically significant main effect, $F(4, 1282.502) = 235.419, p < 0.0021$. The omega squared (0.26) indicated that 26 percent of the total variation in factor scores for this discourse was attributable to register difference. Post hoc comparisons indicated that (1) this discourse was present significantly more in federal DOE webtexts than regional newspapers (Cohen's $d = 0.947$), national newspapers (Cohen's $d = 0.92$), and comments (Cohen's $d = 1.554$) – all large effect sizes; (2) this discourse was present significantly more

---

[3] This includes additional analyses not conducted for this study.

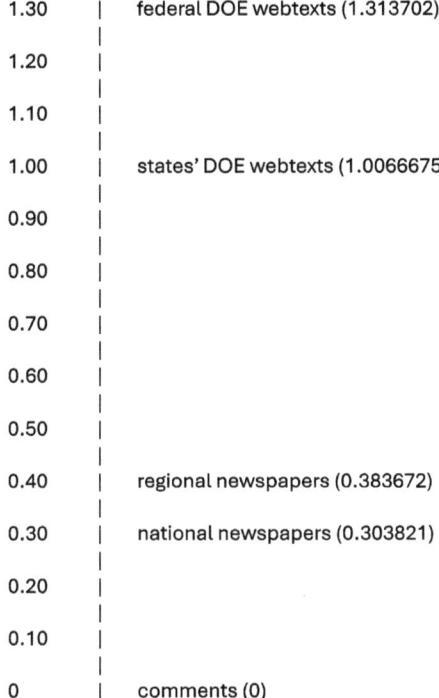

Figure 3 Mean register factor scores for *Government programs serve children in need*.

Factor scores have been adjusted so that lowest mean score is set to 0.

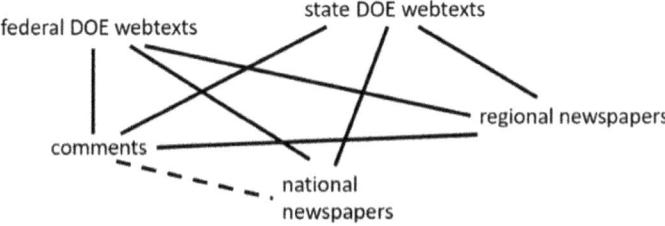

Figure 4 Significant differences and their effects sizes for *Government programs serve children in need* among registers.

Solid lines = large effect sizes. Dashed lines = intermediate effect sizes.

in state DOE webtexts than regional newspapers (Cohen's $d = 0.84$), national newspapers (Cohen's $d = 0.895$), and comments (Cohen's $d = 1.552$) – all large effect sizes; (3) this discourse was present significantly more in regional newspapers than comments (Cohen's $d = 0.815$) (a large effect size); and (4)

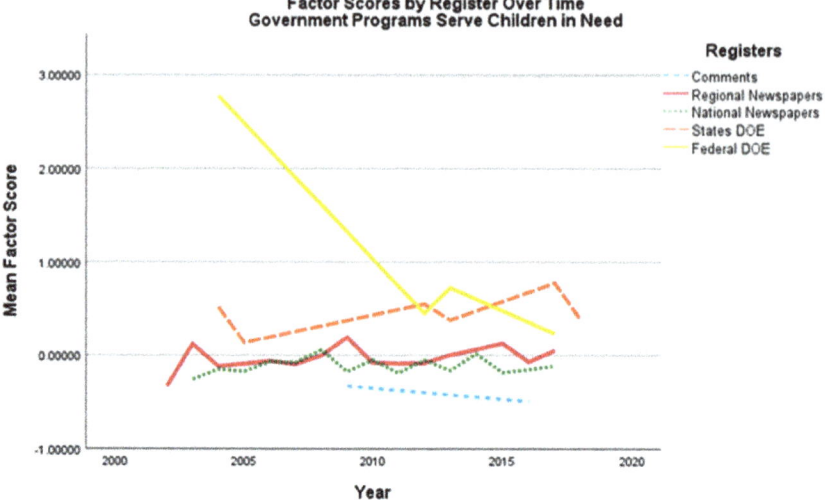

Figure 5 Factor scores by register over time for *Government programs serve children in need*.

this discourse was present significantly more in national newspapers than comments (Cohen's $d = 0.702$) – an intermediate effect size.

5.3.1.2 Variation Over Time by Register

Next, a one-way ANOVA was run to examine whether the factor scores for this discourse were a function of time for comment texts. The independent variable was time (2009, 2016) and the dependent variable was the factor score for each of the comment texts ($n = 1,469$). The test revealed a statistically significant main effect, $F(1,1467) = 52.405$, $p < 0.0021$. Investigation of the mean differences between 2009 and 2016 indicated that, on average, this discourse was present significantly less in the 2016 comments than the 2009 comments on average (Cohen's $d = 0.378$) – a small effect size.

A two-way ANOVA was then conducted to examine the effects of time and register on factor scores for *Government programs serve children in need* for all newspaper texts ($n = 1,436$). The independent variables in this analysis were time (2003–17) and register (regional newspapers, national newspapers), while the dependent variable was the factor score for this discourse for each text. The results indicated no significant main effect for time, nor an interaction effect, but a significant main effect for register, $F(1,1406) = 13.634$, $p < 0.0021$. Investigation of the mean differences between regional and national newspapers indicated that, on average, this discourse was present significantly more in regional newspapers than national newspapers, but that there was no effect (Cohen's $d = 0.169$).

The last analysis in the investigation of register and time patterns in the distribution of *Government programs serve children in need* was a two-way ANOVA with time (2004–5, 2012–13, 2017–18) and register (state DOE, federal DOE) as independent variables. The results indicated a significant main effect for time: $F(2,898) = 108.864$, $p < 0.0021$; register: $F(1,898) = 70.072$, $p < 0.0021$; as well as significant interaction between time and register: $F(2,898) = 109.773$, $p < 0.0021$. Approximately 13.3 percent ($\omega^2 = 0.13$) of the total variance of the factor scores for this ideological discourse was attributable to the interaction of time and register.

Because the interaction between time period and register was significant, the simple main effects of both time and register were examined. There was a significant difference among the three time periods for federal DOE texts, $F(2,898) = 166.033$, $p < 0.025$. Pairwise comparisons of the average factor scores for federal DOE texts for each of the three time periods indicate that this discourse was present significantly more in 2004–5 than 2012–13 (Cohen's $d = 1.542$; large effect size) and 2017–18 (Cohen's $d = 1.999$; large effect size) and that it was present significantly more in 2012–13 than 2017–18 (Cohen's $d = 0.398$; small effect size). That is, this discourse decreased significantly and with a large effect over time in the federal DOE webtexts. There were significant differences for register for the 2004–5 texts, $F(1, 898) = 223.410$, $p < 0.0167$ and the 2017–18 texts, $F(1,898) = 20.307$, $p < 0.0167$. Pairwise comparisons of the average factor scores indicated that this discourse was present significantly more in federal DOE webtexts than state webtexts in 2004–5 (Cohen's $d = 1.678$; large effect size) and this discourse was present significantly more in state DOE webtexts than federal DOE webtexts in 2017–18 (Cohen's $d = 0.48$; small effect size).

In sum, this ideological discourse was most pronounced in DOE webtexts and least pronounced in comments. Its expression decreased over time across all five registers, most precipitously in the federal webtexts between the 2004–5 and 2012–13 time periods.

5.3.2 Immigrant Lives are Narratives (Usually Criminal or Uplifting)

The lexical items *was*, *said*, *had*, *his*, *were*, and *officials* index this ideological discourse in the narrative texts. The narratives present an immigrant subject as either criminal or inspirational in 74 percent of the cases – indicating strong limits on the tropes available within this discourse.

Example 2
The interim United States attorney for the Northern District of New York, **said** the business owner would be deported after serving **his** sentence of 46

months because he **was** an illegal immigrant. ... State **officials** said [NAME] worked on asbestos-removal projects throughout the state ... His lawyer, [NAME], **said**, "He accepted responsibility for his criminal actions."

5.3.2.1 Variation in Register Distribution

First, a one-way ANOVA was conducted to examine the relationship between register and representation of the ideological discourse, *Immigrant lives are narratives (usually criminal or uplifting)*. Figure 6 shows the average factor scores per register for this ideological discourse. Figure 7 shows significant differences and the effect sizes of those differences among the five registers for this ideological discourse. Figure 8 shows the factor scores for each register over time. The test revealed a statistically significant main effect, $F(4, 1480.124) = 614.710, p < 0.0021$. The omega squared (0.40) indicated that approximately 40 percent of the total variation in average factor scores for

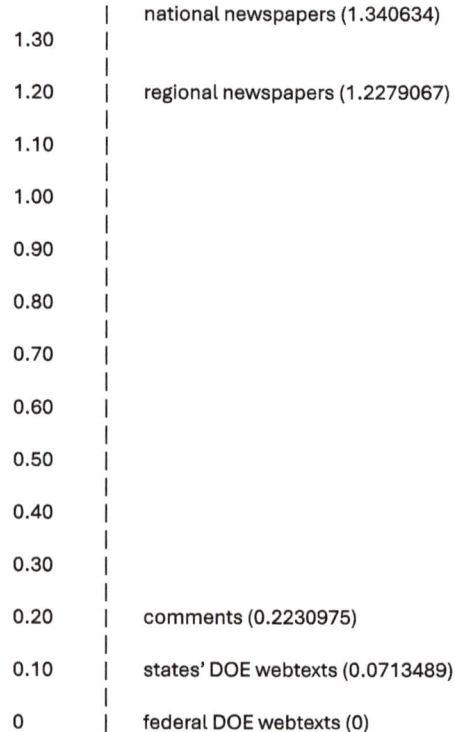

Figure 6 Mean register factor score for *Immigrants' lives are narratives (usually criminal or uplifting)* by register.

Factor scores have been adjusted so that the lowest mean score is set to 0.

Lexical Multidimensional Analysis 63

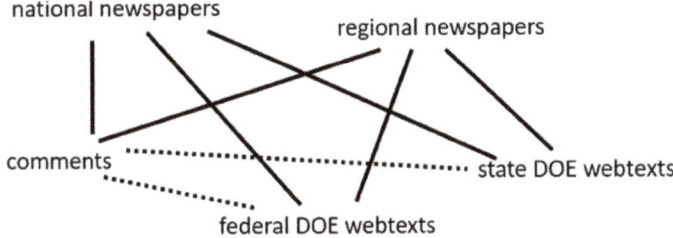

Figure 7 Significant differences and their effect sizes for *Immigrants' lives are narratives (usually criminal or uplifting)* among registers. Solid lines = large effect sizes. Dotted lines = small effect sizes.

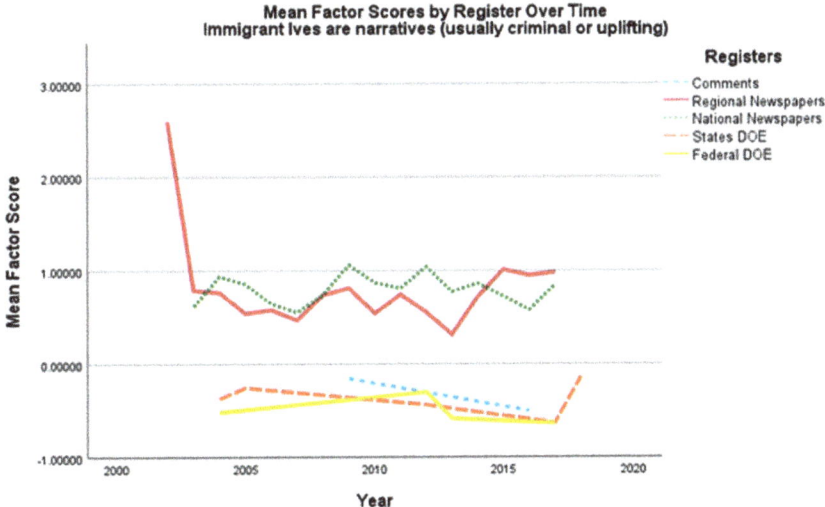

Figure 8 Factor scores by register over time for *Immigrant lives are narratives (usually criminal or uplifting)*

this discourse was attributable to register difference. Post hoc comparisons indicated that this discourse was present significantly more in national newspapers than comments (Cohen's d = 1.618), state DOE webtexts (Cohen's d = 1.916), and federal DOE webtexts (Cohen's d = 2.058) – large effects. In addition, this discourse was present significantly more in regional newspapers than comment texts (Cohen's d = 1.42), state DOE webtexts (Cohen's d = 1.65), and federal DOE webtexts (Cohen's d = 1.77) on average – all large effects. Finally, this discourse was present significantly more in comment texts than state DOE webtexts (Cohen's d = 0.251) and federal DOE webtexts (Cohen's d = 0.373) – both small effects.

5.3.2.2 Variation Over Time by Register

Next, a one-way ANOVA examined whether the factor scores for this discourse were a function of time for comment texts. The test revealed a statistically significant main effect, $F\ (1,1467) = 113.211$, $p < 0.0021$. Investigation of the mean differences between 2009 and 2016 indicated that, on average, this discourse was present significantly less in the 2016 comments than the 2009 comments on average (Cohen's $d = 0.556$) – an intermediate effect size.

A two-way ANOVA was conducted to understand the effects of time (2003–17) and register (regional and national newspapers) on the distribution of *Immigrant lives are narratives (usually criminal or uplifting)*. The results of the two-way ANOVA indicate no significant effects for interaction, time, or register.

Finally, a two-way ANOVA was conducted to understand the effects of time period (2004–5, 2012–13, 2017–18) and DOE registers (federal DOE webtexts, state DOE webtexts) on the distribution of this ideological discourse. The results indicated no significant main effect for register, nor an interaction effect, but a significant main effect for time period, $F\ (2, 898) = 12.706$, $p < 0.0021$. Investigation of the mean differences between the three time periods indicated that this discourse was present significantly more in 2004–5 than 2017–18 (Cohen's $d = 0.412$) and in 2012–13 than 2017–18 (Cohen's $d = 0.279$). That is, this discourse decreased over time in DOE webtexts – though the effect sizes for the decrease were small.

These results indicate a very strong register effect, with newspapers expressing *Immigrant lives are narratives (usually criminal or uplifting)* significantly more than comments or DOE webtexts. While the discourse was stable over time in newspapers, it did decrease over time in both comments and DOE texts.

5.3.3 Top-Down Immigration Laws are Punitive or Permissive

This ideological discourse was expressed using the lexical items *law*, *federal*, *enforcement*, *status*, *officials*, *legal*, *laws*, *undocumented*, and *illegal* to present an immigration law as either punitive for or permissive of immigrants.

> **Example 3**
> Among other things, the **law** requires police to check the immigration **status** of suspects and turn **illegal** immigrants over to **federal** authorities. It requires school **officials** to demand birth certificates from students enrolling for the first time ... proponents are already hailing the **law** as an example of "attrition through **enforcement**."

5.3.3.1 Variation in Register Distribution

As with the other ideological discourses, a one-way ANOVA was conducted to examine the relationship between register and representation of the ideological discourse, *Top-down immigration laws are punitive or permissive*. Figure 9 shows the average factor score per register for this ideological discourse. Figure 10 shows significant differences and the effect sizes of those differences among the five registers for this ideological discourse. Figure 11 shows the factor scores for each register over time. The test revealed a statistically significant main effect, $F(4, 1312.618) = 115.379$, $p < 0.0021$. The omega squared (0.127) indicated that approximately 12.7 percent of the total variation in average factor scores for this discourse was attributable to register difference. Post hoc comparisons indicated that this discourse was present significantly more in regional newspapers than comment texts (Cohen's $d = 0.924$; large effect), state DOE webtexts (Cohen's $d = 0.593$; intermediate effect), federal DOE webtexts (Cohen's $d = 0.527$; intermediate effect), and national newspapers (Cohen's $d = 0.214$; small effect). In addition, this discourse was present significantly more in national newspapers than comment texts (Cohen's $d = 0.771$; intermediate effect), state DOE webtexts (Cohen's $d = 0.421$; small effect), and federal DOE webtexts (Cohen's $d = 0.348$; small effect). Finally, this discourse was present significantly less in comment texts than state DOE webtexts (Cohen's $d = 0.271$) and federal DOE webtexts (Cohen's $d = 0.475$) – both small effects.

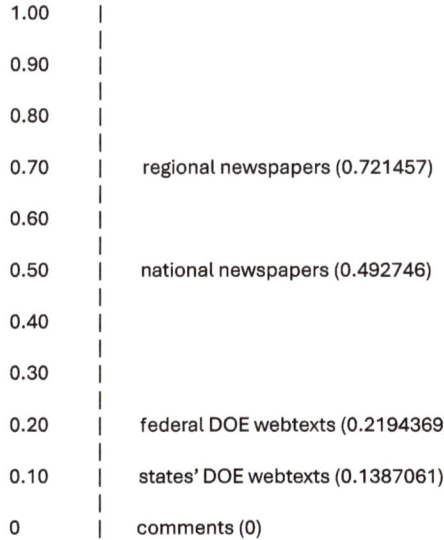

Figure 9 Mean factor scores for *top-down laws are punitive or permissive* by register.

Factor scores have been adjusted so that lowest mean score is set to 0.

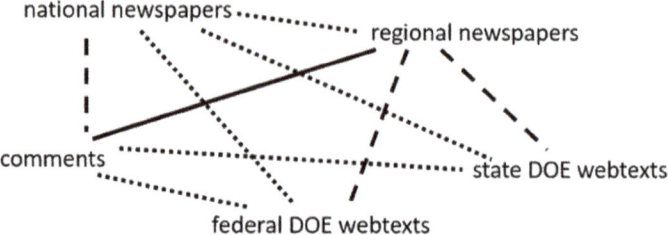

Figure 10 Significant differences and their effects sizes for *top-down laws are punitive or permissive* among registers.

Solid lines = large effect sizes. Dashed lines = intermediate effect sizes. Dotted lines = small effect sizes.

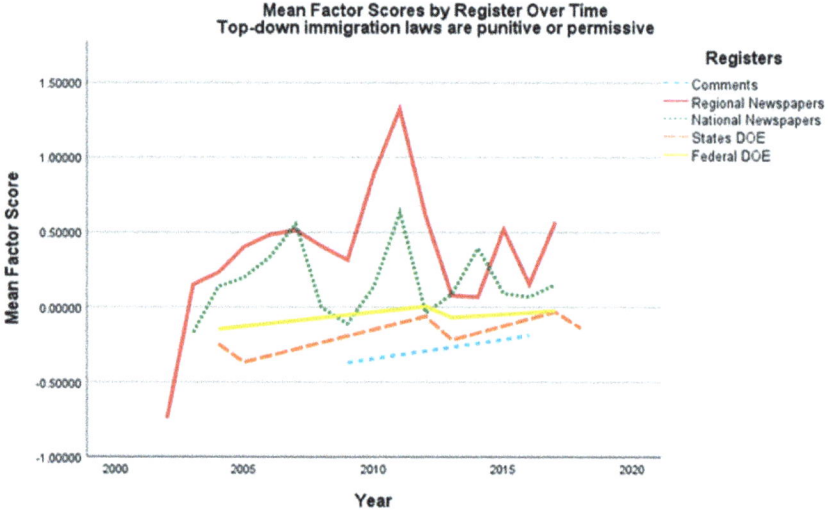

Figure 11 Factor scores by register over time for *Top-down immigration laws are punitive or permissive*.

5.3.3.2 Variation Over Time by Register

Next, a one-way ANOVA examined whether the factor scores for this discourse were a function of time for comment texts. The test revealed a statistically significant main effect, $F(1,1467) = 58.276$, $p < 0.0021$. Investigation of the mean differences between 2009 and 2016 indicated that this discourse was present significantly more in the 2016 comments than the 2009 comments on average for this register though the effect size (Cohen's $d = 0.399$) was small.

The two-way ANOVA conducted to understand the effects of time (2003–17) and register (regional and national newspapers) on the distribution of *Top-down immigration laws are punitive or permissive* indicated no significant effect for interaction but significant main effects for time, $F(1,1406) = 4.155, p < 0.0021$ and register, $F(1,1406) = 19.417, p < 0.0021$. Post hoc tests indicated that this discourse was present significantly more in newspaper texts in 2011 than in 2003 (Cohen's $d = 0.665$), 2004 (Cohen's $d = 0.641$), 2009 (Cohen's $d = 0.646$), 2013 (Cohen's $d = 0.701$), and 2016 (Cohen's $d = 0.682$) – all intermediate effects with the exception of 2013. Looking at the means for register indicates that this discourse was present significantly more on average in regional newspapers than national newspapers, though the effect size was small (Cohen's $d = 0.214$).

The two-way ANOVA conducted to understand the effects of time period (2004–5, 2012–13, 2017–18) and register (federal DOE webtexts, state DOE webtexts) on the distribution of *Top-down immigration laws are punitive or permissive* indicated no significant effects for interaction, or register, but a significant main effect for time period, $F(2,898) = 6.551, p < 0.0021$. Post hoc tests indicated that this discourse was present significantly more in 2017–18 in the DOE webtexts on average than in 2004–5 but that the effect size (Cohen's $d = 0.316$) was small.

Overall, *Top-down immigration laws are punitive or permissive* was expressed significantly more in newspapers than DOE webtexts and comments, and more in regional newspapers than national newspapers. The representation peaked in newspapers in 2011, at the same time that several states passed noteworthy immigration laws. Over time, the discourse was used significantly more often in comments and DOE webtexts.

5.3.4 Immigrants and Governments Have a Mutual Relationship Founded on Acts of Service and Work

The lexical items *served, center, state, number, comprehensive, working*, and *enrolled* indexed this ideological discourse which occurred in texts such as obituaries and online comments and presented scenarios in which immigrants received government support, which was later repaid through labor or service to the state.

> **Example 4**
> The son of immigrant Italian parents, [REDACTED] was first in his family to attend college and obtain advanced degrees. He ... later taught in the same high school from which he had graduated. [REDACTED] helped support his parents by **working** as a letter carrier. . . he ultimately **served** as Bureau Chief for Secondary School Supervision.

5.3.4.1 Variation in Register Distribution

A one-way ANOVA examined the relationship between register and representation of the ideological discourse, *Immigrants and governments have a mutual relationship founded on acts of service and work*. Figure 12 shows the average factor scores per register for this ideological discourse. Figure 13 shows significant differences and the effect sizes of those differences among the five registers for this ideological discourse. Figure 14 shows the factor scores for each register over time. The test revealed a statistically significant main effect, $F(4,1234.458) = 84.700, p < 0.0021$. The omega squared (0.109) indicated that approximately 10.9 percent of the total variation in average factor scores for this discourse was attributable to register difference. Post hoc comparisons indicated that this discourse was present significantly more in federal DOE webtexts than state DOE webtexts (Cohen's $d = 0.658$; intermediate effect size), comments (Cohen's $d = 0.907$; large), national newspapers (Cohen's $d = 0.513$; intermediate effect size); and regional newspapers (Cohen's $d = 0.524$; intermediate effect size). In addition, this discourse was present significantly more in regional newspapers than comment texts (Cohen's $d = 0.656$; intermediate effect size) and state DOE webtexts (Cohen's $d = 0.568$; intermediate). Finally, this

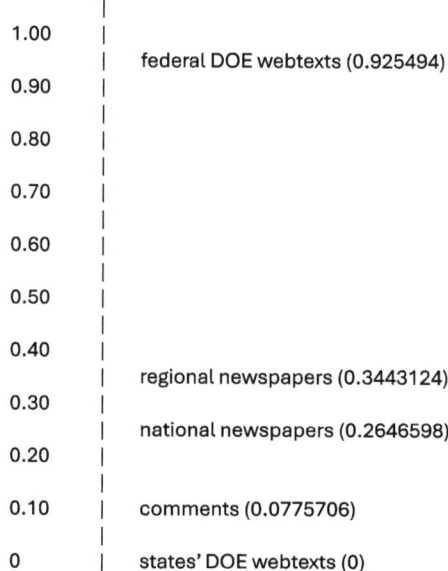

Figure 12 Mean factor scores for *Immigrants and governments have a mutual relationship founded on acts of service and work* by register.

Factor scores have been adjusted so that lowest mean score is set to 0.

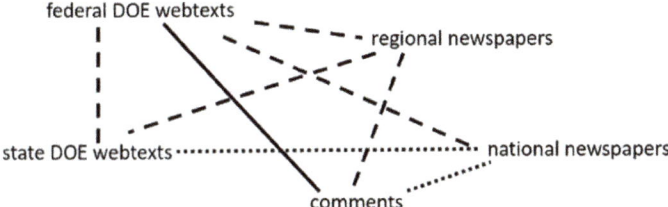

Figure 13 Significant differences and their effects sizes for *Immigrants and governments have a mutual relationship founded on acts of service and work* among registers.

Solid lines = large effect sizes. Dashed lines = intermediate effect sizes. Dotted lines = small effect sizes.

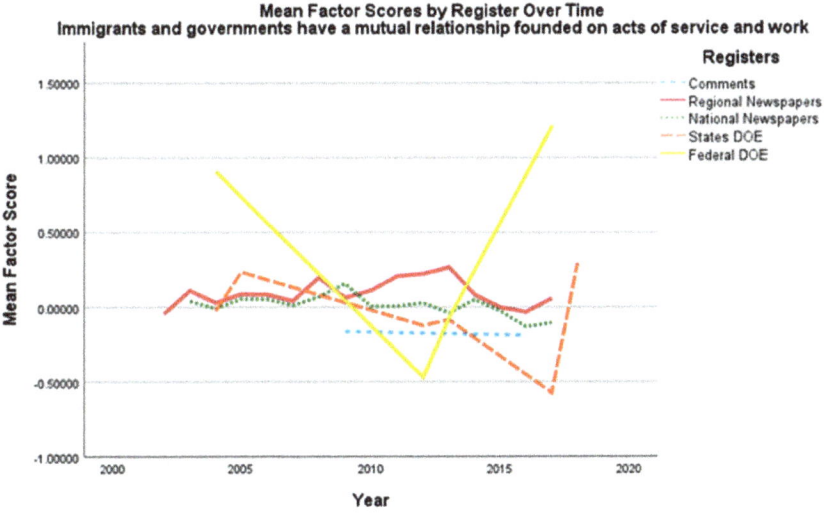

Figure 14 Factor scores by register over time for *Immigrants and governments have a mutual relationship founded on acts of service and work*.

discourse was present significantly more in national newspapers than state DOE webtexts (Cohen's $d = 0.402$; small effect size) and comment texts (Cohen's $d = 0.472$; small effect size).

5.3.4.2 Variation Over Time by Register

A one-way ANOVA to investigate whether the factor scores for this discourse were a function of time for comment texts found no significant differences. That is, there was no change in the level of presentation of *Immigrants and governments have a mutual relationship founded on acts of service and work* over time in the comment texts.

Next, a two-way ANOVA examined the effects of time (2003–17) and register (regional newspapers, national newspapers) on factor scores for *Immigrants and governments have a mutual relationship founded on acts of service and work* for newspaper texts. The results indicated no significant main effect for time, nor an interaction effect. A significant main effect for register, $F(1,1406) = 9.931$, $p < 0.0021$ was identified. Investigation of the mean differences between regional and national newspapers indicated that, on average, this discourse was present significantly more in regional newspapers than national newspapers, but that there was no effect (Cohen's $d = 0.017$).

Finally, a two-way ANOVA was conducted to understand the effects of time period (2004–5, 2012–13, 2017–18) and register (federal DOE webtexts, state DOE webtexts) on the distribution of this discourse. The test indicated a significant interaction effect, $F(2,898) = 34.573$, $p < 0.0021$; a significant main effect for time period $F(2,898) = 14.732$, $p < 0.021$, and a significant main effect for register $F(1,898) = 78.822$, $p < 0.0021$. Approximately 5.9 percent ($\omega^2 = 0.0589$) of the total variance of the factor scores for this ideological discourse was attributable to the interaction of time and register.

Because the interaction between time period and register was significant, the simple main effects of both time and register were examined. For time period, to control for Type 1 error across the two simple main effects for time period, alpha was set at 0.025. There was a significant difference among the three time periods for federal DOE texts, $F(2,898) = 50.596$, $p < 0.025$; and for state DOE webtexts, $F(2,898) = 5.938$, $p < 0.025$. Pairwise comparisons of the average factor scores for federal DOE texts for each of the three time periods indicated that this discourse was present significantly more in 2004–5 than 2012–13 (Cohen's $d = 1.301$; large effect size) and that it was present significantly more in 2017–18 than 2012–13 (Cohen's $d = 0.762$; intermediate effect size). That is, this discourse decreased significantly from 2004–5 to 2012–13 and then increased significantly from 2012–13 to 2017–18 in federal DOE webtexts. Pairwise comparisons for the state DOE texts for each of the three time periods indicated that this discourse was present significantly more in 2004–5 than 2017–18 (Cohen's $d = 0.578$; intermediate effect size) and also significantly more in 2012–13 than 2017–18 (Cohen's $d = 0.459$; small effect size). That is, it decreased significantly over time in state DOE texts. For the register simple main effect (i.e., the differences between state and federal DOE webtexts at each time period), to control for Type 1 error across the three time periods, alpha was set at 0.0167. There were significant differences for register for the 2004–05 texts, $F(1,898) = 26.768$, $p < 0.0167$ and the 2017–18 texts, $F(1,898) = 170.553$, $p < 0.0167$. Pairwise comparisons of the average factor scores indicated that this discourse was present significantly more in federal DOE webtexts than state webtexts in 2004–5 (Cohen's $d = 1.094$) and this discourse was present significantly more in federal DOE webtexts than state DOE webtexts in 2017–18 (Cohen's $d = 0.97$) – both large effect sizes.

Thus, *Immigrants and governments have a mutual relationship founded on acts of service and work* was present significantly more in federal DOE texts than other register types and fluctuated greatly between time periods in this register – decreasing for the texts from the Obama administration. While the representation stayed stable over time in the newspaper and comment registers, it did decrease over time in the state DOE webtexts (i.e., it did not rebound in 2017–8 in state DOE texts as it did in federal DOE texts).

In sum, the sixteen analyses across all four ideological discourses revealed multiple noteworthy findings. There were significant and meaningful differences in the distribution of each of the four focal ideological discourses attributable to register. Furthermore, consideration of time and register together revealed significant though often less pronounced changes over time within particular registers for each of the four focal ideological discourses.

5.4 Discussion

The major cross-cutting finding of this analysis is that register plays an important role in the distribution of ideological discourses about migrant education in this dataset such that different discourses are more prominent in different registers. Across the four ideological discourses, register accounted for 11–40 percent of the variance in factor scores. *Government programs serve children in need* was most prominent in DOE webtexts, particularly federal webtexts. *Immigrants and governments have a mutual relationship founded on acts of service and work* was more prominent in federal DOE texts in the 2004–5 and 2017–18 time frames. *Immigrant lives are narratives (usually criminal or uplifting)* was more prominent in newspapers. *Top-down immigration laws are punitive or permissive* was more prominent in newspapers – particularly regional newspapers. In terms of immigration discourses, these findings suggest that the DOE texts drive the discourses involving government support, while the discourses prominent in newspapers frame entities related to immigration into good/bad binaries. Based on this data, comments do not drive immigration discourses. That register plays an important role in the distribution of ideological discourses is supported by Hoey's (2005) theory of lexical priming, which proposes that a bottom-up lexical priming process which both results from and supports collocational and other lexical co-occurrence patterns is sensitive to situational and thus register contexts. Furthermore, this finding suggests that Biber (2012) might add discourses as a level of language for which register plays an important role as a variational catalyst.

This analysis also found that time contributed to the distribution of ideological discourses. Of note, the time effects in this study tended to be smaller than the register effects and were often moderated by register. Newspapers were the most stable register in this analysis. Comment texts demonstrated change but small effect sizes, and federal DOE webtexts showed the most change over time. These last trends are somewhat counterintuitive as one might expect newspapers to be nimble sources of production and, conversely, bureaucracies to be inflexible. However, when considering the situational context of production, it may be the case that the daily (or even continuous) rate of production for newspapers actually promotes ideological stasis, as journalists and editors may rely on existing lexical choices and issue framings when writing under time constraints. Conversely, while governmental institutions such as DOEs tend to be thought of as bureaucratic and slow to change, in the US, they are arms of elected officials (US president and state governors) and thus, in part, political entities, which may account for ideological change over various administrations.

Finally, this analysis identified some limited interaction effects between register and time, as well as evidence of ideological flow. Two interaction effects were identified, both between the federal and state DOE webtexts. These interaction effects inform descriptions of ideological flow – how the ideological discourses move across time and register. Across the findings of the study, several hypotheses about ideological flow were generated. One observation is that national and regional newspapers may "pull" each other. That is, there are several years for which the slope of discourse change in one newspaper register is then replicated in the slope of the discourse change in the other newspaper register the following year. For example, for *Immigrant lives are narratives (usually criminal or uplifting)* the discourse increased from 2010–11 in regional newspapers and decreased in national newspapers. However, in 2011–12, the discourse increased in national newspapers by the same amount it increased the year before in regional newspapers, while it decreased in the regional papers. Of note, the following year, 2012–13, the discourse decreased in national newspapers by the same amount it decreased the previous year in regional newspapers. Thus, for this time period and this ideological discourse, regional newspapers seem to be "pulling" national newspapers. Another observation from this data is that large changes in one register (e.g., newspapers or

DOE webtexts) seem to be followed by smaller changes later in other registers. For example, *Top-down immigration laws are punitive or permissive* increased with large effect sizes in both newspaper registers from 2009–11. This was followed by increases with small effect sizes in all three of the other registers in the years that followed. Finally, while there were significant changes over time for comment texts for three of the four ideological discourses, the size of the changes were smaller than in other registers and they never led the change, suggesting the hypothesis that ideological discourses in public opinion texts may follow the lead of more institutional sources.

5.5 Conclusion

This case study demonstrates that LMDA is a powerful approach for scaling up and extending studies of ideological discursive constructs. Because it used corpus linguistics methods, large bodies of language data made up of large numbers of texts can be analyzed systematically and quickly, in contrast to many other methodological approaches applied to ideology and discourse studies. Because LMDA produces quantifiable values (e.g., factor scores, factor loadings), it can be used in designs with independent variables (e.g., time, register) and provide information about the significance as well as relative proportion of patterns identified. More broadly, once identified, LMDA provides a data-based way to trace ideological constructs in texts/corpora. It also allows researchers to capture different indexical faces of constructs (i.e., different lexical co-occurrence patterns) across registers as singular constructs. That is, if the same ideological discourse is realized through different lexical choices in different registers, as would be expected (Berber Sardinha, 2017; Hoey, 2005), these multiple realizations are captured as one underlying construct, but analyzable by register through LMDA.

Finally, it is challenging to draw overarching conclusions about the general mood toward migrant education during this time since the findings showed not only a number of nuanced discourses, but also register and time-specific patterns that varied by ideological discourse. That said, the findings do indicate that, over time and register the discursive environment regarding migrant education in the US was aligned with trends of political polarization, as *Top-down immigration laws are punitive or permissive* increased in distribution over time across all five registers at the same time that migrant students might be losing government support, as indicated by a decrease in *Government programs serve children in need* in the federal DOE texts. Altogether, this case study showcases the potential of LMDA to empirically document a highly complex, naturalized landscape of circulating ideological discourses on a topic of social import. The complexity of the findings is not altogether unsurprising given the range of registers sampled, time frames explored, and breadth of perspectives held among such a large populace.

6 Conclusion

In this Element, we have presented the LMDA approach for the exploration of ideological discourses in corpora. We have grounded the approach in conceptualizations of ideological discourses, theories of lexis, and studies of variation from the Flagstaff School of Corpus Linguistics. In terms of technique, we have explained the derivation of the approach from traditional multidimensional analysis and presented guidelines to the reader for conducting an LMDA. We have examined the current body of studies using LMDA, presenting patterns and trends across them. For detailed exemplars, we have shared two case studies – one extracting discourses from a corpus using LMDA and the second analyzing variability in time and register distribution of ideological discourses as an LMDA extension.

This Element has illuminated the potential of the LMDA approach. A key potential lies in the ability to detect socially powerful lexically based constructs in linguistic data at scale. Because, in LMDA, the detection is based on statistical analysis, the resulting ideological discourses have quantitative representations and can thus be further explored in follow-up analyses (e.g., analyses of variance or canonical correlation analysis). An additional potential of LMDA is the ability to "recognize" different lexical manifestations of the same discourse or ideology in different texts. That is, while the identified discursive constructs include multiple lexical variables, only some of these variables are used in specific texts to index the discourse or ideology. Therefore, LMDA allows researchers to both identify the underlying construct (e.g., discourses) and the different representations (e.g., manifestations in particular texts), as well as to investigate patterns in those representations (e. g., register associations).

Based on the LMDA studies conducted thus far, we believe there are a number of fruitful future directions for the approach. Over the breadth of studies conducted using TMDA across languages, registers, and modalities, evidence for potential "universal" dimensions of functional variation have been identified (Biber, 1995). It would, therefore, be interesting to know if there are any "universal" discourses/ideologies. If so, they should be identifiable via LMDA. Furthermore, since the underlying discursive constructs identified via LMDA are operationalizations of sets of quantitative values assigned to a set of lexical variables, it might then be possible to identify these constructs in comparable corpora using the quantitative values.

In sum, this Element has presented rationale for, steps for, and exemplars of conducting LMDA studies to investigate ideological discourses in corpora. We hope this inspires further exploration and innovative applications of this approach.

References

Baker, P. (2010). *Sociolinguistics and Corpus Linguistics*. Edinburgh: Edinburgh University Press.

Baker, P. (2014). *Using Corpora to Analyze Gender*. London: Bloomsbury.

Baker, P. (2016). The shapes of collocation. *International Journal of Corpus Linguistics*, *21*(2), 139–164.

Baker, P. (in press). Corpus-assisted discourse analysis. In C. Chapelle (Ed.), *The Encyclopedia of Applied Linguistics* (2nd ed.). Hoboken, NJ: Wiley.

Baker, P., & T. McEnery. (2015). Who benefits when discourse gets democratized? Analysing a Twitter corpus around the British *Benefits Street* debate. In P. Baker & T. McEnery (Eds.), *Corpora and Discourse Studies: Integrating Corpora and Discourse* (pp. 244–265). London: Palgrave Macmillan.

Bates, D. (2017). The "red door" controversy – Middlesbrough's asylum seekers and the discursive politics of racism. *Journal of Community and Applied Social Psychology*, *27*(2), 126–136.

Berber Sardinha, T. (2014). On being American and Brazilian in Google Books: A multidimensional perspective – Looking at cultural shifts in English over time: A multi-dimensional perspective. Paper presented at the American Association for Corpus Linguistics (AACL) Conference, Flagstaff, AZ.

Berber Sardinha, T. (2017). Lexical priming and register variation. In M. Pace-Sigge & K. Patterson (Eds.), *Lexical Priming: Applications and Advances* (pp. 190–230). Amsterdam: John Benjamins.

Berber Sardinha, T. (2019). Using multi-dimensional analysis to detect representations of national culture. In T. Berber Sardinha & M. Veirano Pinto (Eds.), *Multi-dimensional Analysis: Research Methods and Current Issues* (pp. 231–258). London: Bloomsbury.

Berber Sardinha, T. (2020). A historical characterisation of American and Brazilian cultures based on lexical representations. *Corpora*, *15*(2), 183–212.

Berber Sardinha, T. (2021). Discourse of academia from a multi-dimensional perspective. In E. Friginal & J. Hardy (Eds.), *The Routledge Handbook of Corpus Approaches to Discourse Analysis* (pp. 298–318). Abingdon: Routledge.

Berber Sardinha, T. (2022a). Corpus linguistics and historiography: Finding the major discourses in the first 50 years of TESOL Quarterly. *Journal of Research Design and Statistics in Linguistics and Communication Science*, *7*(1), 69–90.

Berber Sardinha, T. (2022b). Corpus linguistics and the study of social media: A case study using multi-dimensional analysis. In A. O'Keeffe & M. McCarthy (Eds.), *The Routledge Handbook of Corpus Linguistics* (2nd ed., pp. 656–674). New York: Routledge.

Berber Sardinha, T. (2022c). A text typology of social media. *Register Studies*, *4*(2), 138–170.

Berber Sardinha, T. (2023). Detecting macro-discourses around the coronavirus pandemic in large corpora [online plenary talk]. 12th International Conference on Corpus Linguistics (CILC2021), University of Malaga.

Berber Sardinha, T. (2024). Exploring multimodal corpora in the classroom from a multidimensional perspective In P. Crosthwaite (Ed.), *Corpora for Language Learning: Bridging the Research–Practice Divide* (pp. 25–36). Abingdon: Routledge.

Berber Sardinha, T. (to appear). Corpora. In R. Reppen, L. Goulart, & D. Biber (Eds.), *Cambridge Handbook of English Corpus Linguistics*. Cambridge: Cambridge University Press.

Berber Sardinha, T., Delfino, M. C. N., & Collentine, J. G. (2022). Exploring a large corpus of English pop music from a multimodal perspective using lexical MD analysis. CEPRIL Talks: Lexical multidimensional analysis webinar, CEPRIL, Pontifical Catholic University of São Paulo.

Berber Sardinha, T., Romeiro, Y. T. D., Marcondes, L. N. L., Silva, C. S. d., Gerciano, N. P., Kauffmann, C., Pinto, P. T., Dutra, D., Delfino, M. C. N., Bocorny, A., & Sarmento, S. (2023). The coronavirus infodemic: A multidimensional, discourse-based perspective. Panel presented at the Corpus Linguistics 2023 International Conference, Lancaster, UK.

Berber Sardinha, T., & Veirano Pinto, M. (Eds.). (2019). *Multi-dimensional Analysis: Research Methods and Current Issues*. London: Bloomsbury Academic.

Biber, D. (1988). *Variation across Speech and Writing*. Cambridge: Cambridge University Press.

Biber, D. (1993a). Co-occurrence patterns among collocations: A tool for corpus-based lexical knowledge acquisition. *Computational Linguistics*, *19*(3), 531–538.

Biber, D. (1993b). Representativeness in corpus design. *Literary and Linguistic Computing*, *8*(4), 243–257.

Biber, D. (1995). *Dimensions of Register Variation: A Cross-Linguistic Comparison*. Cambridge: Cambridge University Press.

Biber, D. (2012). Register as a predictor of linguistic variation. *Corpus Linguistics and Linguistic Theory*, *8*(1), 9–37.

Biber, D., & Conrad, S. (2004). Corpus-based comparisons of registers. In C. Coffin, A. Hewings, & K. O'Halloran (Eds.), *Applying English Grammar: Functional and Corpus Approaches* (pp. 40–56). Abingdon: Routledge.

Biber, D., & Conrad, S. (2009). *Register, Genre, and Style.* Cambridge: Cambridge University Press.

Biber, D., & Conrad, S. (2019). *Register, Genre, and Style* (2nd ed.). Cambridge: Cambridge University Press.

Biber, D., Conrad, S., & Reppen, R. (1998). *Corpus Linguistics: Investigating Language Structure and Use.* Cambridge: Cambridge University Press.

Blinder, S., & Allen, W. L. (2016). Constructing immigrants: Portrayal of migrant groups in British national newspapers, 2010–2012. *International Migration Review, 50*(1), 3–40.

Bourdieu, P. (1991). *Language and Symbolic Power.* Cambridge, MA: Harvard University Press.

Brezina, V., McEnery, A., & Wattam, S. (2015). Collocations in context: A new perspective on collocation networks. *International Journal of Corpus Linguistics, 20*(2), 139–173.

Caldas-Coulthard, C. R., & Coulthard, M. (1996). Preface. In C. R. Caldas-Coulthard & M. Coulthard (Eds.), *Texts and Practices: Readings in Critical Discourse Analysis* (pp. xi–xii). Abingdon: Routledge.

Cini, M. (2000). Organizational culture and reform: The case of the European Commission under Jacques Santer (EUI Working Papers, 2000/25). San Domenico: European University Institute.

Clarke, I. (2024). The discourses of climate change denialism across conspiracy and pseudoscience websites. In S. M. Maci, M. Demata, M. McGlashan, & P. Seargeant (Eds.), *The Routledge Handbook of Discourse and Disinformation.* Abingdon: Routledge.

Clarke, I., Brookes, G., & McEnery, T. (2022). Keywords through time: Tracking changes in press discourse of Islam. *International Journal of Corpus Linguistics, 27*(4), 399–427.

Clarke, I., McEnery, T., & Brookes, G. (2021). Multiple Correspondence Analysis, newspaper discourse and subregister: A case study of discourses of Islam in the British press. *Register Studies, 3*(1), 144–171.

Cortes, V., & Csomay, E. (2015). Douglas Biber and the Flagstaff School of corpus-based research: An introduction. In V. Cortes & E. Csomay (Eds.), *Corpus-Based Research in Applied Linguistics: Studies in Honor of Douglas Biber* (pp. xv–xx). Amsterdam: John Benjamins.

References

Crossley, S., & Louwerse, M. M. (2007). Multi-dimensional register classification using bi-grams. *International Journal of Corpus Linguistics*, *12*(4), 453–478.

Crossley, S., Varner, L. K., & McNamara, D. (2014). A multi-dimensional analysis of essay writing: What linguistic features tell us about situational parameters and the effects of language functions on judgments of quality. In T. Berber Sardinha & M. Veirano Pinto (Eds.), *Multi-dimensional Analysis 25 Years on: A Tribute to Douglas Biber* (pp. 344–411). Amsterdam: John Benjamins.

Danesi, M. (2017). *The Semiotics of Emoji*. London: Bloomsbury.

Davies, M. (2021). The Coronavirus Corpus: Design, construction, and use. *International Journal of Corpus Linguistics*, *26*(4), 583–598.

Delfino, M. C. N., Berber Sardinha, T., & Collentine, J. G. (2023). Dimensões de variação lexical e acústica na música popular em inglês: um estudo baseado em corpus [Lexical and acoustic dimensions of variation in popular music in English: A corpus-based study]. *Cadernos de Estudos Linguísticos*, *65*, e023025. https://periodicos.sbu.unicamp.br/ojs/index.php/cel/article/view/8671801/33021.

van Dijk, T. A. (2006). Ideology and discourse analysis. *Journal of Political Ideologies*, *11*(2), 115–140.

Egbert, J. (2019). Corpus design and representativeness. In T. Berber Sardinha & M. Veirano Pinto (Eds.), *Multi-dimensional Analysis: Research Methods and Current Issues* (pp. 27–42). London: Bloomsbury.

Egbert, J., & Biber, D. (2019). Incorporating text dispersion into keyword analyses. *Corpora*, *14*(1), 77–104.

Egbert, J., Biber, D., & Gray, B. (2022). *Designing and Evaluating Language Corpora: A Practical Framework for Corpus Representativeness*. Cambridge: Cambridge University Press.

Egbert, J., & Staples, S. (2019). Doing multi-dimensional analysis in SPSS, SAS, and R. In T. Berber Sardinha & M. Veirano Pinto (Eds.), *Multi-dimensional Analysis: Research Methods and Current Issues* (pp. 125–144). London: Bloomsbury.

Ellis, N. (2019). Essentials of a theory of language cognition. *The Modern Language Journal*, *103*, 39–60.

Fairclough, N. (2003). *Analysing Discourse: Textual Analysis for Social Research*. Abingdon: Routledge.

Field, A. (2013). *Discovering Statistics Using IBM SPSS Statistics*. Thousand Oaks, CA: Sage.

Firth, J. R. (1957/1968). A synopsis of linguistic theory, 1930–55. In F. R. Palmer (Ed.), *Selected Papers of J. R. Firth 1952–59* (pp. 168–205). London: Longmans.

Fitzsimmons-Doolan, S. (2014). Using lexical variables to identify language ideologies in a policy corpus. *Corpora*, *9*(1), 57–82.

Fitzsimmons-Doolan, S. (2019). Language ideologies of institutional language policy: Exploring variability by language policy register. *Language Policy*, *18*(2), 169–189.

Fitzsimmons-Doolan, S. (2023). Twenty-first century ideological discourses about US migrant education that transcend registers. *Corpora*, *18*(2), 143–173.

Forchtner, B. (2013). Critical discourse analysis. In C. Chapelle (Ed.), *The Encyclopedia of Applied Linguistics* (pp. 1439–1446). Hoboken, NJ: Wiley.

Fowler, R. (1996). On critical linguistics. In C. R. Caldas-Coulthard & M. Coulthard (Eds.), *Texts and Practices* (pp. 231–249). London: Routledge.

Friginal, E., & Hardy, J. (2019). From factors to dimensions: Interpreting linguistic co-occurrence patterns. In T. Berber Sardinha & M. Veirano Pinto (Eds.), *Multi-dimensional Analysis: Research Methods and Current Issues* (pp. 145–164). London: Bloomsbury.

Friginal, E., & Hardy, J. A. (2014). Conducting multi-dimensional analysis using SPSS. In T. Berber Sardinha & M. Veirano Pinto (Eds.), *Multi-dimensional Analysis, 25 Years on: A Tribute to Douglas Biber* (pp. 298–316). Amsterdam: John Benjamins.

Gabrielatos, C., & Baker, P. (2008). Fleeing, sneaking, flooding: A corpus analysis of discursive constructions of refugees and asylum seekers in the UK press, 1995–2005. *Journal of English Linguistics*, *36*(1), 5–38.

Gal, S. (2018). Discursive struggles about migration: A commentary. *Language and Communication*, *59*, 66–69.

Gillings, M., Mautner, G., & Baker, P. (2023). *Corpus-Assisted Discourse Studies*. Cambridge: Cambridge University Press.

Gorsuch, R. L. (2015). *Factor Analysis*. New York: Routledge.

Gray, B. (2013). Interview with Douglas Biber. *Journal of English Linguistics*, *41*(4), 359–379.

Haroche, C., Henry, P., & Pecheux, M. (1971). La Semantique et la coupure saussurienne: Langue, langage, discours. *Langages*, *6*(24), 93–106.

Haye, A., & Larraín, A. (2018). Field and utterance: The problem of discourse articulation / Campo e enunciado: problema da articulação do discurso. *Bakhtiniana*, *13*(2), 75–93.

Hoey, M. (2005). *Lexical Priming: A New Theory of Words and Language*. Abingdon: Routledge.
Hoffmann, A. J. (2011). The culture and discourse of climate skepticism. *Strategic Organization*, *9*(1), 77–84.
Hunston, S. (2007). Semantic prosody revisited. *International Journal of Corpus Linguistics*, *12*(2), 249–268.
Hunston, S. (2011). *Corpus Approaches to Evaluation: Phraseology and Evaluative Language*. New York: Routledge.
Jaworska, S., & Kinloch, K. (2018). Using multiple data sets. In C. Taylor & A. Marchi (Eds.), *Corpus Approaches to Discourse: A Critical Review* (pp. 110–129). New York: Routledge.
Kauffmann, C., & Berber Sardinha, T. (2021). Brazilian Portuguese literary style. In E. Friginal & J. Hardy (Eds.), *The Routledge Handbook of Corpus Approaches to Discourse Analysis* (pp. 354–375). Abingdon: Routledge.
Keller, D., Gray, B., Smith, J., & Cotos, E. (2022). Zero-inflated factor analysis for short-text multi-dimensional analysis: An MD of rhetorical moves in research articles. Paper presented at the American Association for Corpus Linguistics (AACL) Conference, Flagstaff, AZ.
Krieg-Planque, A. (2010). *A noção de "fórmula" em análise do discurso: Quadro teórico e metodológico* [The notion of "formula" in discourse analysis: Theoretical and methodological framework]. São Paulo: Parábola.
Kroskrity, P. V. (2004). Language ideologies. In A. Duranti (Ed.), *A Companion to Linguistic Anthropology* (pp. 110–129). Malden, MA: Blackwell.
Lo Bianco, J. (2008). Tense times and language planning. *Current Issues in Language Planning*, *9*(2), 155–178.
Marchi, A. (2018). Dividing up the data: Epistemological, methodological and practical impact of diachronic segmentation. In C. Taylor & A. Marchi (Eds.), *Corpus Approaches to Discourse: A Critical Review* (pp. 174–196). New York: Routledge.
Mautner, G. (2005). The entrepreneurial university: A discursive profile of a higher education buzzword. *Critical Discourse Studies*, *2*(2), 95–120.
Murakami, A., Thompson, P., Hunston, S., & Vajn, D. (2017). 'What is this corpus about?' Using topic modelling to explore a specialised corpus. *Corpora*, *12*(2), 243–277.
Orpin, D. (2005). Corpus linguistics and Critical Discourse Analysis. *International Journal of Corpus Linguistics*, *10*(1), 37–61.
Partington, A. (2004). "Utterly content in each other's company": Semantic prosody and semantic preference. *International Journal of Corpus Linguistics*, *9*(1), 136–156.

Partington, A. (2010). Modern diachronic corpus-assisted discourse studies (MD-CADS) on UK newspapers: An overview of the project. *Corpora, 5* (2), 83–108. https://doi.org/10.3366/E1749503210000407.

Partington, A., Duguid, A., & Taylor, C. (2013). *Patterns and Meanings in Discourse: Theory and Practice in Corpus-Assisted Discourse Studies (CADS)*. Amsterdam: John Benjamins.

Pearson, K. (1900). Mathematical contributions to the theory of evolution. VII. On the correlation of characters not quantitatively measurable. *Philosophical Transactions of the Royal Society of London. Series A, Containing Papers of a Mathematical or Physical Character, 195*, 262–273.

Pecheux, M. (1982). *Language, Semantics and Ideology – Stating the Obvious*. London: Macmillan Press.

Peréz-Paredes, P., Aguado Jiménez, P., & Sanchéz Hernández, P. (2017). Constructing immigrants in UK legislation and administration informative texts: A corpus-driven study. *Discourse & Society, 28*(1), 81–103.

Phillips, M. (1985). *Aspects of Text Structure: An Investigation of the Lexical Organisation of Text*. Amsterdam: North-Holland.

Santa Ana, O., Trevino, S. L., Bailey, B., & de Necochea, A. (2007). A May to remember: adversarial images of immigrants in US newspapers during the 2006 policy debate. *Du Bois Review, 4*(1), 207–232.

Schieffelin, B. B., Woolard, K. A., & Kroskrity, P. V. (1998). *Language Ideologies: Practice and Theory*. Oxford: Oxford University Press.

Schmid, H. (1994). Probabilistic part-of-speech tagging using decision trees. *Proceedings of International Conference on New Methods in Language Processing, 12*.

Scott, M. (2016). *WordSmith Tools*. Version 7. Stroud: Lexical Analysis Software.

Silverstein, M. (1998). The uses and utility of ideology: A commentary. In B. B. Schieffelin, K. A. Woolard, & P. V. Kroskrity (Eds.), *Language Ideologies: Practice and Theory* (pp. 123–148). Oxford: Oxford University Press.

Stewart, C. O., Pitts, M. J, & Osborne, H. (2011). Mediated intergroup conflict: The discursive construction of "illegal immigrants" in a regional U.S. newspaper. *Journal of Language and Social Psychology, 30*(1), 8–27.

Stubbs, M. (1996). *Text and Corpus Analysis: Computer-Assisted Studies of Language and Culture*. Oxford: Blackwell.

Stubbs, M. (1997). Whorf's children: Critical comments on Critical Discourse Analysis (CDA). In A. Ryan & A. Wray (Eds.), *Evolving Models of Language* (pp. 100–116). Clevedon: Multilingual Matters.

Stubbs, M. (2001). *Words and Phrases: Corpus-Based Studies of Lexical Semantics*. Abingdon: Routledge.

Stubbs, M. (2009). The search for units of meaning: Sinclair on empirical semantics. *Applied Linguistics*, *30*(1), 115–137.

Stubbs, M. (2015). The textual function of lexis. In N. Groom (Ed.), *Corpora, Grammar, & Discourse: In Honor of Susan Hunston* (pp. 97–115). Amsterdam: John Benjamins.

Taylor, C. (2014). Investigating the representation of migrants in the UK and Italian press. *International Journal of Corpus Linguistics*, *19*(3), 368–400.

Taylor, C. (2018). Similarity. In C. Taylor & A. Marchi (Eds.), *Corpus Approaches to Discourse: A Critical Review* (pp. 97–115). New York: Routledge.

Taylor, C. (2021). Metaphors of migration over time. *Discourse & Society*, *32*(4), 463–481.

van Dijk, T. A. (2018). Discourse and migration. In R. Zapata-Barrero & E. Yalaz (Eds.), *Qualitative Research in European Migration Studies* (pp. 227–245). Berlin: Springer.

Webster, G. (2003). Corporate discourse and the academy: A polemic. *Industry and Higher Education*, *17*(2), 85–90.

Widdowson, H. G. (1995). Discourse analysis: A critical view. *Language and Literature*, *4*(3), 157–172.

Wodak, W., & Meyer, M. (2009). Methods of critical discourse analysis (2nd ed.). London: Sage.

Xu, T., Demmer, R. T., & Li, G. (2020). Zero-inflated Poisson factor model with application to microbe read counts. *Biometrics*, *77*(1), 91–101.

Acknowledgments

Tony Berber Sardinha acknowledges the financial support of the following organizations: São Paulo Research Foundation (FAPESP), Grant #2022/05848-7; National Council for Scientific and Technological Development (CNPq), Grants #310140/2021-8, 420180/2022-2; Coordination for the Improvement of Higher Education Personnel (CAPES), Grant #0245/2022.

Shannon Fitzsimmons-Doolan acknowledges the financial support of this project from the Division of Research and Innovation and the English Department at Texas A&M-Corpus Christi.

To Marilisa and Julia
(TBS)
To Stephen and Annabelle
(SFD)

Cambridge Elements

Corpus Linguistics

Susan Hunston
University of Birmingham

Professor of English Language at the University of Birmingham, UK. She has been involved in Corpus Linguistics for many years and has written extensively on corpora, discourse, and the lexis-grammar interface. She is probably best known as the author of *Corpora in Applied Linguistics* (2002, Cambridge University Press). Susan is currently co-editor, with Carol Chapelle, of the Cambridge Applied Linguistics series.

Advisory Board
Professor Paul Baker, *Lancaster University*
Professor Jesse Egbert, *Northern Arizona University*
Professor Gaetanelle Gilquin, *Université Catholique de Louvain*

About the Series
Corpus Linguistics has grown to become part of the mainstream of Linguistics and Applied Linguistics, as well as being used as an adjunct to other forms of discourse analysis in a variety of fields. It continues to become increasingly complex, both in terms of the methods it uses and in relation to the theoretical concepts it engages with. The Cambridge Elements in Corpus Linguistics series has been designed to meet the needs of both students and researchers who need to keep up with this changing field. The series includes introductions to the main topic areas by experts in the field as well as accounts of the latest ideas and developments by leading researchers.

Cambridge Elements

Corpus Linguistics

Elements in the Series

Doing Linguistics with a Corpus: Methodological Considerations for the Everyday User
Jesse Egbert, Tove Larsson and Douglas Biber

Citations in Interdisciplinary Research Articles
Natalia Muguiro

Conducting Sentiment Analysis
Lei Lei and Dilin Liu

Natural Language Processing for Corpus Linguistics
Jonathan Dunn

The Impact of Everyday Language Change on the Practices of Visual Artists
Darryl Hocking

Analysing Language, Sex and Age in a Corpus of Patient Feedback: A Comparison of Approaches
Paul Baker and Gavin Brookes

Shaping Writing Grades: Collocation and Writing Context Effects
Lee McCallum and Philip Durrant

Corpus-Assisted Discourse Studies
Mathew Gillings, Gerlinde Mautner and Paul Baker

Collocations, Corpora and Language Learning
Paweł Szudarski

Programming for Corpus Linguistics with Python and Dataframes
Daniel Keller

Lexical Multidimensional Analysis: Identifying Discourses and Ideologies
Tony Berber Sardinha and Shannon Fitzsimmons-Doolan

A full series listing is available at: www.cambridge.org/EICL

www.ingramcontent.com/pod-product-compliance
Ingram Content Group UK Ltd.
Pitfield, Milton Keynes, MK11 3LW, UK
UKHW050445210225
455254UK00018B/291